Sunderland at War
1939–45

Sunderland at War 1939–45

Craig Armstrong

PEN & SWORD HISTORY

AN IMPRINT OF PEN & SWORD BOOKS LTD
YORKSHIRE – PHILADELPHIA

First published in Great Britain in 2020 by
Pen & Sword Military
An imprint of
Pen & Sword Books Ltd
Yorkshire – Philadelphia

ISBN 978 1 47389 1 258

A CIP catalogue record for this book is
available from the British Library.

Printed by CPI Group (UK) Ltd, Croydon CR0 4YY

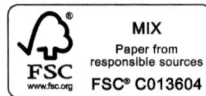

MIX
Paper from
responsible sources
FSC
www.fsc.org   FSC® C013604

Pen & Sword Books Limited incorporates the imprints of Atlas, Archaeology,
Aviation, Discovery, Family History, Fiction, History, Maritime, Military,
Military Classics, Politics, Select, Transport, True Crime, Air World,
Frontline Publishing, Leo Cooper, Remember When, Seaforth Publishing,
The Praetorian Press, Wharncliffe Local History, Wharncliffe Transport,
Wharncliffe True Crime and White Owl.

For a complete list of Pen & Sword titles please contact
PEN & SWORD BOOKS LIMITED
47 Church Street, Barnsley, South Yorkshire, S70 2AS, England
E-mail: enquiries@pen-and-sword.co.uk
Website: www.pen-and-sword.co.uk

Or

PEN AND SWORD BOOKS
1950 Lawrence Rd, Havertown, PA 19083, USA
E-mail: Uspen-and-sword@casematepublishers.com
Website: www.penandswordbooks.com

To my Parents

Contents

Introduction

❖

Sunderland was an important town with a large number of notable industrial concerns. Mining was one of the key industries and Sunderland's port was vital for a great deal of the export of coal from the Durham coalfield.

The coal industry also led to the development of important glass works in Sunderland. The two most famed manufacturers in the town were Turnbull's Cornhill Flint Glassworks at Southwick and the firm of James A. Jobling & Co Ltd (which had been founded as the Wear Flint Glassworks but was renamed in 1921).

The River Wear, and by extension, Sunderland, had a well-earned reputation for shipbuilding and repairing, especially of merchant vessels. This was to prove vital to the nation's war effort and was one of the key reasons for marking the area out as a target of especial interest to the enemy. Firms such as W. Doxford & Sons Ltd., Joseph L. Thompson & Sons Ltd, Sir James Laing & Sons Ltd., Short Brothers Ltd., W. Pickersgill & Sons Ltd., Bartram & Sons Ltd., S.P. Austin & Son Ltd., and John Crown & Sons Ltd. were synonymous with the industry and the area. These were all long-established companies which had made it through the terrible years of the depression in the late 1920s and 1930s. A number of other famous and not so famous yards had failed to weather the storm and had been closed during this awful period, the last being William Gray & Co. Ltd.'s Egis Yard, but shipbuilding and repairing remained a key employer in Sunderland at the outbreak of the war.

The firm of Sir James Laing & Sons Ltd. was first established in Sunderland in 1793, but, like most, had struggled during the 1930s. In 1930, the yard had been closed down and the workforce let go except for the apprentices who slowly completed work on a speculative ship named the SS *Dore*. Orders resumed five years later and the firm established a reputation for building tankers in addition to cargo ships. In 1938, the firm built two tankers for Norwegian owners. The two tankers, the *Eidanger* and the *Alar*, formed the basis for the 'Norwegian-type' tanker which the yard (and the Furness yard at Haverton Hill) built throughout the war. Indeed, shortly before the declaration of war the firm completed work on the 12,000 ton tanker MV *British Prudence*.[1]

Short Brothers Ltd. was another famous shipbuilder whose work had stagnated during the 1930s, with the yard being closed on several occasions due to lack of orders. The last of these occasions was in 1938 but the yard was reopened in 1939 and completed two ships that summer: the SS *Hermiston* and the SS *Scorton*, both Maierform tramps for Chapmans, a Newcastle company. This highlighted the speciality of the yard, for Shorts was known as the 'local' yard because of the amount of work it undertook for locally based companies.

Like most north-east communities, Sunderland had experienced great hardship during the depression-haunted days of the late 1920s and 1930s, with the shipbuilding industry being particularly hard hit by the slump. Many men lost their jobs, leaving families struggling to survive in straitened circumstances. By the latter half of the 1930s, the industry was beginning to recover although some yards had now gone for good.

Unlike the yards on the Tyne, the shipyards of Sunderland specialised in the building of merchant vessels and many of the yards also specialised in repairing damaged ships. Both of these specialties would prove to be vital to the national war effort and would mark Sunderland out for special attention from the Luftwaffe.

In addition to the shipbuilding there were numerous ancillary industries which supplied material for the shipyards and many Sunderland men worked in these engineering and industrial firms.

CHAPTER 1

1939: The Breaking Storm

❖

With war now declared, the town's ARP personnel were almost constantly on duty in case of the heavy and instant aerial bombardment, anticipated by most. The wardens were not only expected to protect the community against air attack and to enforce ARP regulations such as the blackout, but were also expected to maintain communications and to report any incidents to higher authority. At this early stage of the war, the wardens were woefully under-equipped and methods of communication were haphazard at best. They were often forced to rely on the civilian telephone system, even though there was every chance that the system would be badly disrupted in the event of an air raid. The wardens were at first a sight which provoked curiosity, humour and often ridicule from some sections of the community, especially the younger members of society who had yet to be evacuated.

Sunderland, like most other communities, had a back-up plan for communications during an air raid, which involved ARP messengers, usually young boys from organisations such as the Boy Scouts. This plan was thrown into some confusion just days into the war, however, when insurance problems resulted in the authorities having to order Boy Scouts younger than 14 to cease any work for the ARP services until further notice. Those aged between 14 and 16 could still undertake such duties with their parents' permission, but would not be used as messengers during a raid.

A Warden at his Post in a Telephone Box, Observed by a Curious Onlooker (Sunderland Echo)

The evacuation scheme in Sunderland got off to a rather stuttering start and it seemed as though the authorities were rather confused over what official intentions were. Delays had resulted in confusion and muddle over when exactly the evacuation would begin and where the evacuated were to be billeted. This disorganised start was in strong contrast to several other communities. Newcastle upon Tyne had launched its evacuation programme on 1 September (before war was actually declared), Tynemouth and Wallsend began its own evacuations on 4 September, as did many other places such as Edinburgh.[2]

The authorities were increasingly concerned over the numbers of those who had been withdrawn from the evacuation lists in recent days. At one Sunderland school, 70 children had been withdrawn from the scheme out of a total of 240 (29 per cent). Those in charge of the evacuation scheme blamed this mass withdrawal on apathy amongst parents who had been lulled into a false sense of security due to the fact that the massive and immediate bombing which had been expected had not occurred. The Evacuation Officer, Mr W. Thompson, told the local press that this was a foolish attitude as the present, largely peaceful, conditions might not continue and the bombing campaign could begin at any time. He therefore urged all parents to consider the safety of their children and to re-register them. Mr Thompson also informed parents that a large rush of children at the last moment would place too much strain on the transport system and that there would be no further evacuations. This meant that if children were not evacuated in the first round of evacuations they would not have another opportunity.

It would seem that some parents had been put off the scheme by a false rumour that they would be expected to pay for the board and lodging of their children if they were evacuated. Mr Thompson told parents that this was completely untrue as the government had promised to take on those costs but then confused the matter somewhat by adding that there was a suggestion that parents who were able to, might voluntarily make a contribution at some future point.

The truth is probably more complex. Many parents would have taken the decision that they could not bear to be parted from their children no matter the risk and preferred to face whatever might come as a family unit. Others may well have been put off by the seemingly chaotic nature of the scheme with muddle and confusion encouraging those who could afford it to arrange the evacuation of their children themselves. Mr Thompson explained that those parents who had arranged for the evacuation of their children themselves would not be eligible for claiming allowances for those who were hosting their children and would have to pay all costs themselves.

Elsewhere, the evacuation had already caused some controversy, with many in the reception areas being horrified by the state of some children from the poorer districts of towns and cities. There had already been some criticism in the national and regional press of the fact that many of these children were poorly dressed, lacked shoes or other items of clothing, had poor manners and were unhealthy, infested, or dirty. Reacting to this, Mr Thompson stated that he was aware of some of these criticisms but, failing to acknowledge the causes behind them, said that 'it is up to parents to see that their children are in a fit state both to travel and to go into a new home' as he 'did not want children from Sunderland to be open to criticism in this respect'.[3]

With the authorities anxiously awaiting news of when the evacuation would begin they alerted parents as to what their children should bring with them when the call came. All children were to come equipped with night clothes, comb and brush, slippers or sandshoes, towel, soap, facecloth, toothbrush, and, if possible, an extra pair of boots or shoes. In addition to this, and the clothes which they were wearing, boys were ordered to bring a vest, a shirt with collar, a pair of underpants, a jersey or pullover, a pair of trousers, handkerchiefs, two pairs of socks or stockings, and a cap, while girls were to bring a vest or combinations, a pair of knickers, a bodice, a petticoat, two pairs of stockings, handkerchiefs, gym slip and blouse, a hat, and a cardigan. All clothing was to have a name tag sewn into it and all children were also to bring a haversack and their gas mask and holder. This list would seem to be wildly optimistic given the fact that many of the children who were to be evacuated came from poorer districts within the town and providing every item on the list (sometimes for several children) would prove to be a severe stretch for many families.

Three days after war had been declared, the authorities in Sunderland finally informed those who had signed up for and were eligible for evacuation that the scheme would begin on Sunday, 10 September. On this first day it was hoped that 15,000–16,000 schoolchildren and other priority cases would be evacuated from the town via the railway stations at Monkwearmouth, Millfield and Pallion.

Even this late on, however, the authorities were unable to inform people which reception areas the evacuees would be sent to or even to give times of departures. The local press informed readers that unofficial reports stated that some 1,200 evacuees from Sunderland would be billeted in Sedgefield rural areas with children being picked up at three stations: Ferryhill, Sedgefield and Trimdon. This area was no stranger to evacuees as its residents had already housed 1,500 evacuees from the Newcastle area.

An evacuation rehearsal was held on 6 September with thousands of children turning out to be briefed and to have their evacuation kits inspected. The rehearsal was intended to ensure that children, staff and helpers were prepared but also that the education authority staff who had organised the scheme were familiar with what needed doing. The experience of one typical school highlighted some of the difficulties inherent in the evacuation scheme. Approximately 80 per cent of the pupils from this school were eligible for evacuation but a large minority were not as they lived on a new housing estate on the outskirts of Sunderland, which fell outside the evacuation scheme. The headmaster, however, was pleased with how the rehearsal went, telling a reporter that although almost all of the children came from poor homes, 'in the majority of cases their kits were in perfect order – obviously the result of considerable care and even sacrifice on the part of their parents'. He acknowledged that some children were short of clothing and that the school had done its best to try to rectify this. At this school, the headmaster had taken it upon himself to brief the parents on what might be expected in advance of the official announcements regarding the evacuation scheme. This had resulted in a spirit of cooperation and also resulted in the children taking the upheaval 'very calm and, indeed, cheerfully'.

The evacuation scheme was to take place over two days with the schoolchildren leaving on the first day and the second day seeing the evacuation of women with children under 5 and other priority cases. Just days before the evacuation, women being

Sunderland evacuees (Unknown)

Sunderland evacuees at Millfield Station (Sunderland Echo)

Sunderland evacuees at the station (Sunderland Echo)

Mother and child evacuees at Millfield Station (Sunderland Echo)

Sunderland evacuee secures a name tag to a much younger evacuee (Sunderland Echo)

Mothers and children being evacuated from Pallion Station (Sunderland Echo)

evacuated with young children were informed that they would not be permitted to take prams with them to the billeting areas and so should leave them behind.

In order to organise this second evacuation the town had been divided into ten areas and people allocated to report to a specific school.

Districts for the Evacuation of Women with Children Under Five and Priority Cases.

District	School
1	Thomas Street
2	Redby
3	Monkwearmouth
4	Valley Road
5	Hendon Infants
6	Hudson Road
7	Cowan Terrace
8	Chester Road
9	Diamond Hall
10	Hylton Road

Most private schools within the town were to reopen in mid-September but classes would take place during the morning and early afternoon with children being responsible for bringing their own lunches. These schools were all to be equipped with their own special air raid shelters and the pupils were to be trained in ARP methods. Some private schools, however, had taken the decision to organise their own evacuation. Rock Lodge School, for example, evacuated itself to Newton Hall Boarding School in Northumberland, while Thornhill Grammar School evacuated staff and pupils to Durham where their classes would take place in the Commercial School. These arrangements were not always of great use. The move to Durham, for example, meant that staff and pupils from Thornhill would be billeted in Durham itself. There was no guarantee that Durham would not itself be a target of the enemy. The High School for Girls had only four pupils who were eligible for evacuation and these were to be sent along with one of the mistresses from the school. At Grange School for Girls there were eighteen pupils eligible for evacuation but in the event only two had submitted their names and the school was to carry on with morning lessons from 21 September. In order to safeguard the staff and pupils, the cellars were to be strengthened and the pupils drilled in ARP methods. Argyll House had also taken the decision to carry on with lessons as it had been inundated with letters from parents asking that the school routine carry on as normal. The school would therefore remain open between 9.00am and 2.00pm. St Anthony's and Montessori schools also took the decision to remain open.

One of the priority cases to be evacuated on the second day of the scheme were the blind. There were an estimated 400 blind people living in the area eligible for evacuation but only 60–70 had indicated that they were going to leave. The manager of Sunderland and Durham County Institution for the Blind, Mr Hugh C. Miller, said that he had spoken with several blind workers and most had told him that they felt they would be just as safe staying in Sunderland and there was a marked and natural reluctance to leave their homes. Mr Miller added that several blind people had made their own arrangements and had left the town in the last few days and he urged any blind people who had initially declined evacuation but had now changed their minds to report to the institution.

One of the other reasons for the evacuation was that many schools were to be commandeered by the local authorities for the use of a variety of ARP services, many being used as emergency rest or feeding centres. At South Hylton, for example, the council schools had been commandeered and converted for use as a dressing station.

Just days after the declaration of war, the authorities at South Hylton declared that their own ARP arrangements were now well advanced with sufficient personnel recruited to allow the system to work adequately. This would seem to have been rather optimistic as there were still shortages of personnel and equipment. The provision of air raid shelters had been especially problematic, with many people not being supplied with suitable shelter at this juncture. Some residents had taken matters into their own hands and had constructed shelters of their own. One enterprising householder had built a shelter which would house himself and nineteen others.

Sunderland's ARP services were also understrength at the outset of the war and on the day that war was declared the mayor made a strong appeal for men and women to offer their services now that their necessity was so obvious. Almost all sections of the ARP services were still understrength and had vacancies for full and part-time volunteers, both male and female. In particular demand were men who were trained in the building industry to work in the rescue squads; men and women to serve as wardens; men for the Auxiliary Fire Service (AFS), and men and women for the casualty services. Those willing to volunteer for the casualty services did not have to be trained, although it would help, as training would be provided. Other volunteers in demand were those men or women who owned and could drive motor vehicles. The mayor was at pains to reinforce the message that although he town's ARP organisational scheme was now completely planned it could not function efficiently without the necessary numbers of volunteers stepping forward to play their part. Those willing to volunteer were encouraged to submit their applications to addresses printed in the local press and those wishing to volunteer for duty as air raid wardens or in the AFS were urged to apply to the police department, Thornholme. Anyone wishing to become a special constable could submit their names at Gill Bridge Avenue police station. There were four choices open to people who wished to serve in the casualty service: both men and women could apply to serve in first aid posts or as ambulance drivers, but the first aid parties were open only to men. All applications could be made to the ARP headquarters at Thornholme. The other choice for the casualty service was for fit men aged 25–50 (building experience an advantage) who could volunteer to serve in the rescue squads by applying to the borough engineer's office at the town hall.

As the country geared up for the coming conflict, there were many changes to ordinary life. With most people expecting fuel to be rationed and the government discouraging unnecessary travel, many motorists made plans to lay up their vehicles for the duration. For others, this was not a option as their vehicles were taken over for national service, especially by the ARP and first aid services. These owners turned their vehicles over to the authorities at local police stations and were offered some compensation.

It was clear that rationing would be put in place and have a severe impact on ordinary life. Preparations for this were already in an advanced stage of planning and more than 150 Sunderland meat traders met at the Palatine Hotel in the first days of the war to discuss the creation of a wartime butchers' association. The deputy meat agent for town and district, Mr S.P. Goodfellow, presided over the meeting. He told his fellow traders that in this time of national crisis it behoved them to pull together and

Motor-vehicle owners turn over the vehicles to the authorities outside a Sunderland police station (Sunderland Echo)

to act in a united way to benefit the whole community rather than work for the advantage of individuals. The National Federation of Meat Traders had urged the creation of Retail Butchers' committees, which would act as bulk-buying groups for all butchers in their areas. The members voted unanimously in favour of forming such a group and elected Mr J. Dinsdale as president. It was agreed that two buying committees would be formed, one for the south side of the river and one for the north.

Councillor R.G. Smart put it to the membership that it might be favourable to consider the earlier closing of their shops, at sunset, as a security measure and economy and this was favourably accepted. Concluding the meeting, the other deputy meat agent, Mr Harry Dixon, explained that he and Mr Goodfellow were also responsible for other outlying areas, including Boldon, Herrington, Houghton-le-Spring, Ryhope and Silksworth, and had already held meetings in these outlying districts.

At the same time as the Retail Butchers' committee was being created, the local authority were also considering matters concerning food supplies. The town council, under the auspices of the general purposes committee, set up a food control committee which would oversee many of the aspects of rationing and the supply of food in the town. The committee comprised fifteen people made up of five representatives of the food trades and ten representing the consumer. The five food trade representatives were: Mr T.M. Stores (representing the grocers and provisions dealers); Councillor R.G. Smart (butchers and fleshers); Mr Robert Whitfield (Co-operative Society); Mr G. Muirhead (fish trade); and Mr J. Earnshaw (bakery trade). The consumer representatives were: the mayor (Councillor Myers Wayman); aldermen Cairns, Embleton and Summerbell; and councillors Crow, Huggins, Semple, Patrick, Bell and Young. The general purposes committee also set up an advisory committee for the rationing of coal, gas and electricity and the Borough Treasurer, Mr F. Wilcox, was appointed as fuel overseer to act in conjunction with the members of the committee.

It was expected that the army might have to base units in the town and that billets would therefore be required for both officers and other ranks. The army council, therefore, set rates for those who accommodated soldiers. This rate was quite complicated but those who billeted soldiers would receive varying amounts depending on whether or not meals were provided. Where meals were furnished the base rate was set at 10*d* per night for the first soldier and a further 8*d* per night for each further soldier. For an officer, pay would be 3*s* per night for the first officer and 2*s* per night for each further officer. Breakfast was 8*d* for each soldier, dinner 11*d*, tea 3*d* and supper 6*d*. For those billets which provided only a bed and no food or food preparation areas, the rates were 6*d* per night for soldiers. Unfurnished accommodation in otherwise occupied premises stood at 2*d* per night, regardless of rank, and half that amount for accommodation in similar but unoccupied premises. The likelihood of having to stable army horses was also a possibility and was accommodated by a similar scale. Stabling with 10 lbs of oats, 12 lbs of hay and 8 lbs of straw per day was priced at 2*s* 3*d* per day per horse. Stabling without forage was paid at a rate of 6*d* per day per horse and where stabling was provided in a building not otherwise used as a stable and without forage the sum was 3*d* per horse per day.

The local authorities also appointed a number of people to the local Billeting Appeals Tribunal. This tribunal would be responsible for hearing cases when people complained over their being listed as being suitable for billeting personnel who had been brought into the area in light of the wartime situation. The tribunals would consist of three people, one of whom would most likely be a woman, who would be appointed on a rota.

One of the biggest and most noticeable changes to everyday life was the immediate imposition of a strict blackout, which was enforced by both the police and the wardens' service. The blackout initially caused some problems as accidents increased and some people found themselves victims of being unable to navigate their way around the blacked-out town. One early victim was a Swedish seaman named Petersen. Mr Petersen (20) had been found wandering drunkenly in the town by a member of the public who had escorted him to the police station where he was arrested for drunkenness and kept in one of the cells overnight for his own safety. The following morning, the unfortunate sailor was fined 6s by Sunderland magistrates.

The mayor, accompanied by representatives of the police and ARP services, had toured the town on the first night of the blackout and had been largely impressed by the fact that the vast majority of residents were complying with the regulations. A substantial minority, however, were not. The mayor singled out licensed houses, fish shops and cinemas as being the group which most flouted the regulations but he also described how some householders had used materials which were quite unsuitable for blacking-out their homes and noted that a significant percentage of motorists and buses were being driven without regard to the blackout regulations. He also emphasised that it was a very serious offence to disobey the blackout regulations and that the police would take immediate and strict action in the future, as from now on there could be no excuse or plea of ignorance for flouting the blackout. Those who did so were endangering not only their own lives but the lives of everyone in the town.

With the war now a reality, many young people decided that this was not a time to wait for the future and this led to a boom in business at Sunderland Registrar's Office, where the staff were inundated with couples wanting to get married. Many were army reservists and territorials who had been called up.

With the vital necessity of maintaining the coastal supply routes along Britain's east coast, especially the coal trade from the northern coalfields to London, the Admiralty, using lessons hard-learned in the First World War, instituted a convoy scheme from 6 September. These convoys were vital to the nation's war effort and many Sunderland men serving in the merchant navy found themselves working on them. By the end of the war there had been some 7,700 convoys around the British coast comprising of approximately 173,000 ships.

On the same day that the convoy system was instigated around the British coast, a ship, which had steamed from Sunderland bound for the River Plate, was intercepted off the north coast of Spain by the U-47. After refusing to stop the SS *Rio Claro*

The SS Rio Claro *(State Library of New South Wales)*

was fired upon and her four-man crew forced to surrender. After being questioned they were put into boats before the U-Boat sank the cargo ship with a torpedo.[4]

At last the day arrived when Sunderland's evacuation scheme was launched with the evacuation of nearly 8,000 schoolchildren from the town on Sunday, 10 September. The children assembled at their schools and were escorted to one of three stations where twenty special chartered trains were awaiting them. The authorities were left disappointed as the total of 7,910 represented only 50 per cent of the approximately 16,000 who, a week previously, had signalled their intention to be evacuated.[5] The number also represented only one-third of the 24,000 children living in the evacuation zone. The ratios of those who took up the offer of evacuation varied widely between different schools with St Hilda's leading the way with 112.8 per cent of those who had registered being evacuated on that first day (i.e. more children were actually evacuated than were registered), while at St Paul's only 28.9 per cent took up the chance.

Ratio of Registered Schoolchildren Evacuated on 10 September 1939.

School	Percentage Evacuated[6]
St Hilda's	112.8
Bede Girls	111.7
Bede Boys	107.8
Junior Technical	105.4
Hendon	89.3
Bishopwearmouth	82.2
Monkwearmouth Central	79.7
St Mary's	79
West Park	76.1
Garden Street	75.9
Hylton Road	72.7
Simpson Street	70.5
St Patrick's	69.7
Commercial Road	68.5
Barnes	68.1
Deptford Terrace	67.7
St Columba's	67.3
Fulwell	67.3
Redby	67.2
St Joseph's	65.2
Diamond Hall	62.6
James Williams Street	62.5
Chester Road	61.7
St Benet's	60
Pallion	59.8
Stansfield Street	57
Grange Park	56.1
Thomas Street	55.1
High Southwick	54.9

Hudson Road	54.8
West Southwick	54.5
Cowan Terrace	50.6
Valley Road	48.6
St John's	47.4
Green Terrace	46
Moor	44.9
St Andrew's	35
Monkwearmouth C of E	34.2
St Paul's	28.9

We have already mentioned some of the reasons for people deciding not to send their children away. In one case an outbreak of measles prevented a large number of children from departing as scheduled. This was at Sunderland Nursery School where only 50 from the expected 100 children departed for Hawthorn Tower, south of Seaham Harbour.

In the event, the officials from the education services described the largest exodus in the town's history as having gone extremely smoothly but there was an undoubted note of sadness prevalent in the atmosphere of the town. Parents cheered light-heartedly but there was clearly a desire that the war end quickly so that families could be reunited. Fortunately, many of the children were too young to understand the full significance of what was happening and although there were some tearful scenes the majority seem to have viewed the start of the day as an adventure. By the time the children boarded the trains, many were tired after having been up early and having had to stand in queues loaded down with their backpacks for several hours. For many, it was their first trip aboard a train.

Those who departed from Monkwearmouth Station were more fortunate as the soldiers of the station's National Defence Company went amongst the youngsters passing out cups of tea. At Millfield Station, parents were forced to wave their children off from the other side of the road as the crowds were so large that the police were forced to keep them back. Many parents were angered at this and some, determined to wave their children off, scaled a 10ft wall which stood beside the western platform. At Millfield, one young girl was seen clutching a huge doll in her arms while a 14-year-old boy played the mouth organ and encouraged friends to sing the South African trek song. Alderman E.E. Embleton, the chairman of the education committee, watched several of the trains depart and stated his pride in the children of Sunderland saying that 'their appearance is a credit to their parents and the town'.[7]

Despite the claims of a smooth operation there were some last-minute problems. At Pallion New Road, a group of evacuees met three platoons of young soldiers marching in the opposite direction and the schoolchildren all halted to watch the soldiers pass by before resuming their journey. More seriously, protests from parents over their children, from Hudson Road and Moor schools, being sent to Horden in Easington Rural District, resulted in the authorities instead agreeing to send them further afield to Bedale, Pocklington and Malton. Two other schools from the same district, St Mary's and St Benet's Catholic schools, were also bound for Horden but the parents here had no problem over this destination.

In many cases children walked to stations but in some other cases the corporation arranged for transport in the form of buses and trams. The busiest station was Millfield, from which eight trains departed between 8.50am and 1.45pm. At Monkwearmouth, six trains left between 8.20am and 1.15pm while six trains also departed from Pallion Station between 8.30am and 2.15pm.

As well as Alderman E.E. Embleton visiting departure stations the mayor, Councillor Myers Wayman, also visited and talked to several groups of evacuees. Councillor Wayman told a newspaper reporter that 'thanks to the splendid organisation, everything went off without a hitch'. The Director of Education, Mr W. Thompson, found time to praise the staff, teachers, helpers, police, railway employees and all others who worked to ensure the smooth running of what was a complex and trying operation. He admitted that while it was obvious that many parents could ill afford everything their children needed for the journey, he could see they had made huge sacrifices to ensure they were all well equipped.

Not every evacuee enjoyed the experience and for two Sunderland families the situation led to embarrassment and unforeseen repercussions. The two lads, aged 13 and 9, had been evacuated to Shotton with the rest of their school and upon arriving had been sent to live in what was described as one of the best homes in the village. They were given a good meal, then went outside to play. After looking around their new home the two had a conversation during which they expressed their lack of satisfaction with the village and its amenities, thinking they would be bored there. There and then they decided to walk back home and arrived, footsore, the next morning having trekked the dozen miles from Shotton. Their parents asked the authorities to take the boys back to their billet but this request was refused and the families were told that either the boys would have to remain in Sunderland or they would have to arrange their own evacuation privately.

As we have seen, the Admiralty was well aware of the threat presented from submarine warfare. After all, Britain had nearly been knocked out of the First World War by unrestricted submarine warfare. Convoy systems were already in place for many, but not all, merchant vessels but the military responses to the threat of the U-Boat menace were rather more problematic. In the first month of the war the Admiralty used fast aircraft carriers escorted by destroyers, organised into hunter-killer groups, to patrol likely areas but this was to prove disastrous and provided Orkney with its first fatalities of the war. On 14 September, the aircraft carrier HMS *Ark Royal* was unsuccessfully attacked by a U-Boat but lessons were not immediately learned and just three days later the converted aircraft carrier HMS *Courageous* was leading its own hunter-killer group in the Western Approaches.[8] During the evening of 17 September she was patrolling off the coast of Ireland when she was called to the assistance of a British merchant vessel which had been attacked. All of *Courageous'* aircraft had landed and she was preparing to launch a fresh wave when she was struck by two torpedoes fired from U-29. All electrical power was immediately lost, and the carrier capsized and sank within twenty minutes of being struck, losing 519 of her crew.

Amongst the dead of HMS *Courageous* were at least two Sunderland men. Stoker 1st Class Joseph Alfred White (25) was the son of Catherine and the late William White and left behind a widow, Alice May White (née Pearson) at their family home in Sunderland. In the days following his death, several tributes were paid in the local press including one from his mother in which the family described how they were grief-stricken.[9] The second casualty was an RAF man serving aboard HMS *Courageous*. Aircraftman 1st Class John George Dixon (24) was the son of Edgar and Mary Ellenor Dixon of Sunderland.[10]

On the same day that the aircraft carrier was lost, another Sunderland merchant seaman lost his life when his vessel fell victim to a U-Boat. The Pallion-built (by the firm of Short Bros. Ltd) SS *Kafiristan* was towards the end of a voyage from Jucaro, Cuba to Liverpool carrying 8,870 tons of sugar. When she was 350 miles off Cape Clear, the cargo ship was attacked by the U-53. The first torpedo fired by the submarine missed but at 4.14pm the submarine administered the coup-de-grace with another torpedo and the cargo ship sank. Twenty-nine of her crew survived the sinking and were rescued later by an American ship and subsequently landed at New York. Six of the crew lost their lives. Amongst them was the Chief Engineer, John James Mason (53). Chief Engineer Mason left his widow, Hannah, at their Sunderland home.[11]

In November, the firm of Joseph L. Thompson & Sons Ltd. launched its first vessel of the war. This was the motor cargo-liner *Port Quebec*. This ship had initially been intended for the Port Line but she was requisitioned by the Admiralty and hurriedly converted into a minelayer carrying approximately 500 mines for setting up mine barrages. In this capacity she served with the 1st Minelaying Flotilla based at Kyle of Lochalsh on the Scottish west coast.[12] During the remainder of the year the yard launched three of its seven wartime Economy types. These were the SS *Argyll*, the SS *Inverness* and the SS *Royal Emblem*.

SS Kafiristan *(Library of Contemporary History, Stuttgart)*

HMS Port Quebec *in military service (Public Domain)*

CHAPTER 2

1940: Darkest Hour

March saw controversy in theatre circles when the 'Queen of Striptease', Phyllis Dixey, starred in the show *Eve Takes a Bow* at the Sunderland Empire. Dixey had joined ENSA and performed songs, recitations, and, most popular of all with the troops, naked tableaux. In the course of *Eve Takes a Bow,* Phyllis performed a striptease dance called *Confessions of a Fan Dancer*. The show was widely attended on 4 March, the opening night. A review of the show in the *Sunderland Echo* of 5 March was positive overall, stating that the large crowd was treated to a show which followed 'familiar lines but, nevertheless, provides sound entertainment'. The reviewer had particular praise for several of the cast of dancers but said that the 'good looks and pleasing personality of Phyllis Dixey could have been used to better advantage in this show than in *Confessions of a Fan Dancer*, which, as is usual with these striptease acts in Sunderland, got a cool reception'.[13] The reviewer went on to praise the music but was disappointed with the comedy aspect of the show.

Some of the more puritan elements of Sunderland society shared the opinion of the reviewer and audience and were appalled at what they saw as a show which lauded a decline in moral standards being permitted in their town. When Miss Dixey took the stage on 6 March, her performance was halted half-way through by the intervention of the police, who ordered

Miss Phyllis Dixey (Telegraph)

the scene to be blacked out. When Miss Dixey objected to this, Chief Constable Cook banned the act altogether. Miss Dixey complained that the actions of the police were hard to understand as she believed there was nothing objectionable in her act and that it 'has been seen in various places in the provinces without the shadow of a disagreeable incident'. She defiantly added that she did not 'propose to alter it out of Sunderland'.[14]

The shipyards of Wearside were now abuzz with activity as government orders flowed in alongside increased numbers of private orders and requests for repair work. Sir James Laing & Sons Ltd. at Deptford had numerous government contracts but also managed to complete the 6,825 ton motor tanker MV *Athelcrest* in April.

The dire situation facing the British merchant fleet was highlighted by the short career of the tanker. In the early hours of 25 August, the MV *Athelcrest* was in convoy 90 miles off the Flannan Isles when she was hit by a torpedo fired from U-48. The torpedo caused catastrophic damage and resulted in a fire, forcing the abandonment of the ship. Thirty crewmen were lost, although the master and five crewmen were rescued by HMS *Godetia*, which then scuttled and sank the stricken tanker. MV *Athelcrest* had survived less than five months of wartime service.

Short Brothers Ltd. was also involved in extensive government work but throughout the course of 1940 found the time to complete four tramps for private owners. These were the SS *Barnby*, the SS *Hazelside*, and two motor tramps for Common Bros. of Newcastle: the MV *Hindustan* and the MV *Newbrough*.

The firm of Joseph L. Thompson & Sons Ltd. produced a further four of its Economy-type tramps in early 1940. These were the SS *Confield*, the SS *Graiglas*, the SS *Thistelgorm*, and the MV *St Esslylt*. After the launch of these vessels the yard was switched to the construction of standard 'Empire' tramps. By the end of the war the yard had built twenty-three of these vessels. One of the reasons for the switch was that, in addition to the prefabricated nature – meaning the ships could be constructed more speedily and with less expertise amongst the workforce – the yard had prior experience with the type, having launched the SS *Dorington Court* shortly before the war began. This ship could carry 10,000 tons of cargo at a steady speed of 11 knots and used only a 2,500hp engine. The *Dorington Court* formed the prototype for thirteen of the Empire tramps built at the yard during the war.

As the battered soldiers of the BEF retreated towards the Dunkirk area, the RAF made desperate attempts to disrupt or even halt the oncoming Nazi forces. The efforts continued day and night and casualties were heavy, especially for the unfortunate bombers operating in daylight. On the morning of 17 May, for example, twelve Bristol Blenheim bombers took off from England to attack enemy tank formations. A failure to meet up with their fighter protection resulted in all but one of the Blenheim's being shot down. Although those airmen operating at night did not have to face the opposition from enemy fighters in so great numbers, the dangers of navigating over unfamiliar, and often heavily defended, territory at night was also a risky proposition and a number of casualties resulted from these sorties. On the night of 21/22 May several squadrons from Bomber Command launched a series of attacks against enemy transport in the Cambrai area. Four of the bombers failed to return. One of these was Wellington IC (*P92998, KO-H*) of 115 Squadron. The Wellington had taken off from RAF Marham at 11.45pm but failed to return and it was later revealed that it had crashed, killing all of the six-man crew. The wireless operator/air gunner aboard the Wellington was a 19-year-old Sunderland man. Aircraftman 1st Class (AC1) John Thomas Packer was the son of William and Mary Alice Packer and lies with his crew at Schoonselhof Cemetery at Antwerp, Belgium.

With the intense air action over France a number of RAF fighter pilots made an early reputation for themselves. Amongst them was Sunderland-born Joseph Robert Kayll. Educated at Aysgarth and Stowe the young man had not shown great commitment to his academic pursuits and, after failing all his exams, had found work, aged 16, as a mill boy at the Sunderland sawmill company of Joseph Thompson. He also learned how to fly planes and obtained his 'A' Licence in 1934 before joining the ranks of the Auxiliary Air Force with 607 (County of Durham) Squadron. A skilled pilot, promotion rapidly followed, and in early 1939 he attended an instructors' course. Upon his return, as a flight lieutenant, he was appointed commander of 'A' Flight and flew to France with the squadron in November 1939.

On 14 March, Kayll was promoted to acting squadron leader and posted to take command of 615 (County of Surrey) Squadron at Vitry. On the following day he was credited with the destruction of two Me 110s, followed by two more enemy aircraft, including an He 111 bomber five days later. Two days after this he claimed another He 111 as probably destroyed and another damaged and, on the final day of the month, he destroyed an Me 109 and claimed another as damaged. After the return of the squadron to Britain, Squadron Leader Kayll was awarded the DSO and DFC, receiving the decorations from the king at RAF Kenley.

In the chaos of the retreat to Dunkirk, many soldiers from the north-east of England were separated from their units and the chaos led to doubts over the dates on which men had lost their lives. The men of the 2nd Battalion, Durham Light Infantry (DLI), were serving with the 2nd Infantry Division and had held German forces at the River Dyle, where the first army Victoria Cross (VC) of the war was awarded to a South Shields man, Second Lieutenant Richard Annand. By late May, the 2nd Division was holding 21 miles of the Dunkirk corridor and managed to hold off no fewer than four Panzer Divisions, although it suffered the loss of 70 per cent of its strength. Amongst the casualties during this nightmarish period was Platoon Sergeant Major Cuthbert Fairclough. A 34-year-old native of Sunderland, PSM Fairclough was obviously an experienced soldier as the rank of PSM was a pre-war experiment which gave command responsibility, usually reserved for commissioned officers, to experienced warrant officers. It was dispensed with in 1940 and most warrant officers in this rank bracket were commissioned as lieutenants. Fairclough was killed between 24 and 25 May and is buried at St Venant Communal Cemetery. The following expression was placed upon his headstone '... WHOSE ACTIVE SERVICE IS NOT ENDED HERE BUT IS RENEWED IN OTHER FIELDS OF DUTY R.I.P.'[15]

We have already encountered the activities of the highly successful Squadron Leader Kayll, DSO, DFC. After his duties in France, his score stood at five confirmed victories along with one probable and several damaged. A happy event occurred when Squadron Leader Kayll married Miss Annette L. Nisbet on 9 June. Following the ceremony, several Spitfires of his squadron performed aerobatics over the happy couple.

During the Battle of Britain, 615 Squadron was based at Kenley from 20 May to 29 August and took part in the fighting during the initial convoy battles, the coastal battle of the second phase and the first days of the third and most fiercely fought third phase. Squadron Leader Kayll shared in the shooting down of an He 59 and on 14 August he damaged a Do 17 bomber. He followed this with a He 111 shared on 16 August, an Me 109 damaged two days later, and on 20 August

Squadron Leader Kayll and his Bride (Daily Mirror)

he shared victory over a Do 17. Four days later he shared an He 111 with another, alongside an Me 109, claimed as damaged two days later. Finally, on 28 August, Kayll claimed a Do 17. Withdrawn to northern Scotland for a rest period the squadron was posted to RAF Northolt on 10 October and took part in the final phase of the Battle of Britain. Squadron Leader Kayll claimed an Me 109 damaged on 25 October. On 22 December, Kayll relinquished command of 615 Squadron and was posted to Fighter Command HQ. Reflecting the close nature of the auxiliary squadrons, a relative of Kayll's married one of his colleagues in November. Flight Lieutenant W.F. Blackadder, an Edinburgh man flying with 607 Squadron, married Patricia Kayll of South Hill, the Cedars, Sunderland, at Christ Church,

Flight Lieutenant Blackadder and Miss Kayll (The Tatler)

Sunderland. It is very likely that the two had been introduced to each other when 607 Squadron was based at RAF Usworth at the beginning of the Battle of Britain.[16]

Even as the Battle of Britain raged and the future of the country was in the balance, crime continued to blight Sunderland. At the end of June, the town was shocked by the murder of a 78-year-old widow named Emma Jane Harrison. The elderly woman lived at Wear Street and the police were first alerted to the crime when a report came in from West Hartlepool where a 19-year-old Sunderland soldier named John Charles Mather had walked into the police station and confessed to the crime. Mather was a sapper in the Royal Engineers and his home was at Millum Terrace, Monkwearmouth. Appearing before Sunderland magistrates the chief constable, George H. Cook, explained how detectives had gone to Mrs Harrison's address and upon gaining entry had discovered her body lying in a corner beneath a window. It was clear that the unfortunate woman had been dead for many hours and her body showed the signs of considerable injuries. The detectives took possession of several items, which they believed would be of use as evidence, then visited West Hartlepool where Mather made a statement. At this initial hearing the chief constable asked for the prisoner to be remanded and the magistrates agreed while also furnishing Mather with legal aid. Mather, described as a tall fair-haired young man, did not comment and appeared dressed in civilian clothes.

The case was next heard at Sunderland Police Court on 12 July when the prosecutor, Mr Edward Cope, said that the 'case was a simple and sordid one'. He alleged that Mather, while home on leave, had spent the day of 25 June drinking in a number of public houses, accompanied by his mother and grandmother. During their drinking spree they had borrowed small amounts of money from several neighbours and Mrs Mather had also pawned a blanket. The next morning, his mother spotted Mather leaving her house hurriedly by the back door. He subsequently made his way to the police station at West Hartlepool where he confessed to police that he had killed a woman. Appearing for the prosecution, Dr H.A. Cookson stated that Mrs Harrison had sustained severe head injuries, including a fractured skull, and that the injuries were possibly caused by a coal rake which had been recovered from the scene.

The young soldier's mother, Martha Mather, testified that she, along with her mother, who lived in the same Wear Street tenement property as the victim, had indeed been drinking heavily with her son and that on the night in question they had gone back to her mother's home on Wear Street when her son had said he would 'go and see old Emma and see if she will lend me something'.[17] He had been gone for approximately quarter of an hour before returning, claiming that he got a loan of 4 or

5 shillings. Mrs Mather claimed that she had heard no noises commensurate with a struggle while her son had been absent.

PC Myles of West Hartlepool testified that he had been the first to question Mather and explained how, when he had asked the soldier if he had outstayed his leave was shocked when the young sapper answered that he had killed a woman in Sunderland. Superintendent W. Cook of West Hartlepool added further details. He stated that Mather had said that when he had visited Mrs Harrison he had agreed to rake up her fire for her and while he was doing so the widow began making statements about his mother telling the young soldier that she 'was no good'. He then stated that he had lost his temper and had struck Mrs Harrison on the head with the coal rake. It was also observed that his tunic was splashed with blood.

Detective Sergeant Jermy stated in court that the accused had told him that he did not know why he had acted as he had and that he had been drinking all day. The detective also testified that upon entering Mrs Harrison's room he had found her body, a blood-stained coal rake and two broken knives. Superintendent Middlemist of Sunderland police testified that upon questioning Mather after he had been taken to Sunderland, the soldier had refused to make any comment. The case was referred to Durham Assizes in October.

While the main attention of the British people was focused on the fighter pilots of the Battle of Britain, the men of Bomber Command and Coastal Command were fighting their own bitter conflicts as part of the greater battle. Bomber Command was repeatedly mounting raids on the invasion ports and on German aerodromes, suffering heavy losses in doing so. On the night of 23/24 July, Bristol Blenheim IV (*R3748*) failed to return from an operation to bomb an airfield near Bernburg. No trace was ever found of the crew of the bomber and it is believed that it crashed in the North Sea, killing all three crewmen. The wireless operator/ air gunner in the bomber was Sergeant Israel Winberg. Sergeant Winberg (28) was a Sunderland-born Jewish man who before the war had been a commercial traveller in the furniture trade and had joined the RAF on 5 November 1939. His parents were

Morris and Anna Winberg (née Tinn) but it would appear that at some point either during the war or shortly thereafter the family changed its name to the more English-sounding Winburn.[18]

On the night of 26 July, the Norwegian merchant vessel MS *Balzac* left Sunderland with a cargo of 1,350 tons of coal bound for Cowes on the Isle of Wight. This was a regular trip for the vessel and her crew, it was the third time they had made it, but on this occasion disaster struck. At around 9.00pm the *Balzac* was anchored off Roker light waiting for a convoy when there was an explosion underneath the amidships of the vessel. The ship did have degaussing equipment fitted but this was not working as the engine was stopped at the time of the explosion. The stricken merchant ship broke in two and sank within five minutes. Of the twenty men of the crew, nine were killed. The eleven survivors had jumped overboard, with eight of them, including two gunners from the 1st London Irish Rifles, clinging to a raft. The survivors were picked up by a pilot cutter which was coming out to the vessel at the time. This was because the ship had been guided out by Sunderland pilot George Hall (33) and the pilot vessel was to pick him up and return him to his post. Mr Hall had been in the saloon of the ship along with Captain Knut Johansen at the time of the explosion and both men were amongst those to lose their lives. Mr Hall of the Sunderland Pilotage Authority, Lighthouse and Pilotage Authorities, was the son of Thomas and Isabella Hall and left behind a widow, Mary.[19]

Shortly after 11.00pm on 26 June, the people of Sunderland were awoken by the wail of the air raid sirens as approximately 100 enemy aircraft were detected crossing the Scottish and north-east coast. Shortly after midnight, a high-explosive bomb detonated at Witherwack Farm, Southwick, but this resulted in no casualties or significant damage. Meanwhile, fifty incendiary bombs fell on the village green at Whitburn. Others fell onto a haystack and a house but again, no damage was done.

During the afternoon of 30 June, enemy aircraft were in action off the east coast with the first recorded daylight bombing sortie of the war over Britain taking place at Hull, and action off the coast as other aircraft laid mines or searched for shipping to attack. Eight miles east of Sunderland, a Heinkel He 59 seaplane was attacked and badly damaged by Spitfires. The Heinkel was forced to land on the sea and the crew of four, one of whom was injured, were picked up by a British cruiser. The He 59 was used extensively by the Luftwaffe as a search and rescue aircraft and this one was painted white with clear red crosses and had no armament. The aircraft was beached nearby and inspected. Although this was a violation of the rules of war, the RAF was perfectly justified in taking such action as it was later shown (and widely suspected at the time) that many of the He 59s were being used not only to pick up stranded German crews and return them to the fray but were also monitoring radio transmissions and carrying out reconnaissance of shipping lanes.[20]

No doubt the majority of the Sunderland public could not have cared less about the RAF shooting down German search and rescue aircraft. Many were desperately awaiting news of loved ones who had been posted missing in the chaotic aftermath of the fall of France. The parents of Lance Sergeant Thomas Richardson Davis (29) and Private George Henry Davis (24) must have faced an especially anxious wait as both of their sons had been posted missing within days of each other while serving with the DLI in France.

The elder brother had been a civil servant in Felling before the war and had gone to France with the 6th Battalion, DLI. By the end of July, it had been confirmed that he had survived but been taken as a prisoner of the Germans. Lance Sergeant Davis found himself incarcerated at Stalag 383 at Hohen Fels in Germany. Thomas survived his imprisonment and by early June 1945 he was reported as no longer being a PoW.

Younger brother George had been a regular soldier for seven years before the start of the war and was recalled to the colours at the start of the conflict and posted to France with the 2nd Battalion, DLI. Unfortunately, his parents, Edward and Eleanor, received news that their son had been killed at some date between 21 May and 1 June 1940. It was later confirmed that Private Davis had lost his life on 21 May. He is buried at St Venant Communal Cemetery where his parents had the

inscription 'HIS HEART TO
HIS HOME, HIS LIFE FOR
HIS COUNTRY, HIS SOUL
TO HIS GOD' inscribed upon
his headstone.

On 8 July, a Junkers Ju 88
which was reportedly on a sortie
to Sunderland was shot down
in flames while over Yorkshire,
crashing at Hornsea, killing one of
the crew while the remaining three
were captured after bailing out.

The Luftwaffe continued

Lance-Sergeant Thomas Richardson Davis
(l) and his younger brother, Private George
Henry Davis (r), both posted missing with
the DLI in France (Sunderland Echo)

its campaign to target British
shipping off the east coast but shortly before midnight on the
night of 19 July, the anti-aircraft defences managed to bring
down a four-engine Focke-Wulf Fw 200C 'Condor' maritime
reconnaissance/bomber which was employed on a minelaying
sortie. The big aircraft crashed into the North Sea between
Sunderland and Hartlepool with four of the six-man crew
being killed or missing believed killed. The survivors were taken
prisoner.[21]

On 23 July, there was a tragedy in Sunderland which resulted
in the death of a 4-year-old child from 22 The Parade, Hendon.
Brenda Usher's mother was in hospital while her father was away
in the army and the little girl was being looked after by another
woman who was a family friend. The youngster was going to
buy some *williks* (winkles) with a halfpenny that the woman
looking after her had given her, when she was hit by a lorry.
A witness reported seeing the little girl stumble over the kerb and
into the road in the lorry's path. The lorry driver reacted quickly
to swerve his vehicle and came to a halt within half a length
of his vehicle, but little Brenda was seen to be lying beside the
near front wheel. At the inquest, Coroner Morton said that the
little girl died from shock and multiple head, and other, injuries.
Recording a verdict of accidental death, the coroner added that
it might be of some comfort to the parents to know that the

An Fw 200C Condor similar to the one shot down on the night of 19 July (Bundesarchiv, Bild 146-1978-043-02 / CC-BY-SA 3.0)

woman who was looking after Brenda had not been negligent in any way.

With shortages of many building materials already having an impact on many people, some of the Sunderland public turned to crime in order to secure supplies either to use or to sell on at a premium rate. In late July, three Sunderland boys, two aged 13 and one aged 10, appeared before magistrates at Sunderland Juvenile Court accused of wilful damage to a fence and with stealing £5-worth of timber belonging to Mr Robert Elliott. Called to give evidence, Mr Elliott's brother told magistrates that timber had regularly been going missing from a building site on Seaforth Road that they had been working on since 1 January. Mr William Elliott testified that on 15 July he had reported the theft of more timber to the police and, clearly suspecting that the offenders were certain youths, he had visited the houses of three youths and had recovered timber worth 14s 6d, which had been used in the construction of an air raid shelter and in a garden path.

PC Hunter was the next to testify and he stated that on the following day he had visited the youths, and all had confessed to stealing the timber. No proof could be found that they had been responsible for the earlier thefts and the charges relating to these thefts had therefore been dropped. PC Jordan testified that Mr Elliott had complained to him that a fence of his had been damaged and he had questioned the boys, with one of the 13-year-olds admitting that he had pulled down the fence in company with the other two. Mr J. Taylor, a probation officer, testified that all three boys had been closely associated with each other for some time and that all had been before the court before, with one outstanding fine still remaining unpaid.

The mother of the boy whose fine remained unpaid was questioned by the court and told the chairman, Colonel Laing, that she had forgotten the fine. He remarked that she seemed to forget most things, before accusing her of forgetting 'the education of your son'. All three mothers stated that they had no knowledge that the timber had been stolen and that they believed that it had been picked up on the street, claiming that there were only one or two pieces found during the searches.

Mr William Elliott told magistrates that the majority of the found timber was recovered from the house of one of the boys and only one or two pieces recovered from the remaining two addresses.

Given that the boys were all past offenders it was no surprise that the magistrates decided to inflict a stern punishment on them and their families. For the wilful damage to the fence, the boys were ordered to each pay 2s 6d in damages and the two boys from whose houses little had been recovered were fined 4s 10d each with their parents ordered to pay 5s each. The boy in whose house most of the timber was found was also fined 4s 10d and placed on probation for two years, while his parents were bound over in the sum of £2.

With parental authority waning in the face of wartime conditions and the lack of schooling due to either disruption through evacuation or through the closure of schools, juvenile crime was increasing and was of particular and growing concern to the authorities in Sunderland (and elsewhere). On the same day that the offences above were heard, a boy of 15 was also brought before the Juvenile Court magistrates. The defendant was charged with being found on enclosed premises. Witness Arthur Carlson testified that on Saturday, 20 July he had seen the accused on the roof of a property, a butchers, at 13 North Bridge Street. He had immediately notified the police and he and PC Patton discovered the youth in an outhouse at the rear of the premises. The butcher who owned the shop, Mr Allan, claimed that he had complained in the past of cases of petty pilfering from his shop, where the youth was employed.

Interviewed by the police, the youth had insisted that he had no intention of stealing anything from the premises but was merely looking for somewhere to sleep as he had had a row with his father and did not wish to return home. This defence was brought low when the boy's father testified that no such row had taken place. His case was made worse when magistrates were told that he had been brought before the court on several occasions on various charges, including one of larceny from a slot machine. Sentencing the lad to probation for two years, Colonel L. Laing remarked that the youth had 'a very bad record'.[22]

Another Sunderland youth, John Patrick Armstrong of Peacock Street West, was rather lucky to be shown leniency when he was brought before Sunderland Police Court. He was, at the time, on licence from borstal and the mayor described him as having led a life of petty crime since 1932. On this occasion, Armstrong was accused of stealing 5*s* from the handbag of a woman named Mrs Isobel Harris of Kitchener Street. Somewhat surprisingly, Armstrong's case was adjourned for six months, although he was warned that if he found himself running afoul of the law again during that time he could expect a prison sentence.

Mr Robert Henry Hitchings Wood (18) appeared before the magistrates asking that his driving licence be restored to him. The licence had been removed after he was convicted of several charges of having taken motor vehicles without the owners' consent and driving without third-party insurance. At first, Mr Wood told magistrates that he wished to obtain work as a chauffeur. This rather optimistic plea was, unsurprisingly, refused by the magistrates. Mr Wood then said that he wished to regain his licence so that he could enter RAF service as a driver and was told that if he reappeared before the magistrates giving proof of application to the RAF they might reconsider the matter.

Many Sunderland residents had fallen victim at one time or another to the admonishments of an ARP warden over poor implementation of blackout regulations and there was some resentment to the, at times, overly zealous approach of some wardens. No doubt there would have been smiles and some satisfaction in the news that the wife of a Sunderland warden had been fined the sum of £3 for showing an unobscured light during the blackout. Special Constable Hatcher related to the court how he had been summoned to the premises in Tatham Street where he found a crowd of more than thirty people shouting and creating a disturbance at the front door of the house because a light was showing clearly in a front window. Mrs Florence Johnson did not appear in court but was represented by her husband, a Norwegian man who told magistrates he had been on ARP duty at the time of the offence. Mrs Johnson was one of a raft of people and companies to fall victim to magistrates for blackout breaches at this time. Amongst those fined on the same day were three householders who were each fined the sum of £3 4s and Steel & Co. Ltd. of the Crown Works, Pallion, who were fined a total of £10 on two charges of allowing unobscured lights to be shown from their works.

Trying to run a household in Sunderland during 1940 was an increasingly difficult and stressful activity. Longer work hours, rationing, shortages and queuing all meant that the housewife was increasingly struggling to cope. Housewives were also exposed to large numbers of appeals to save vital supplies and to use materials sparingly. Soap was one such household staple which housewives were repeatedly urged to manage carefully. Some companies were not slow to capitalise on the wartime attitude towards waste and many adverts appeared in local and national newspapers promoting a variety of products which might enable the struggling and increasingly put-upon housewife to manage her household more efficiently and easily. For example, throughout the summer of 1940 adverts appeared for Carbosil water softener which, it was claimed, made soap last far longer.

In the confusion of the fall of France, many Sunderland men had been reported missing and families faced an anxious wait for news of the fate of loved ones. The local press kept people updated and on the first day of August the front page of the *Sunderland Echo* featured eleven men in its regular roll of honour column, seven of whom were reported missing.

Lance Corporal Thomas Davison (39) of High Street East was serving in the Auxiliary Military Pioneer Corps (AMPC) in France when he was reported missing. By October, his family had been informed that he had been taken prisoner in France and was now a prisoner of war. Lance Corporal Davison was later imprisoned at Stalag 8b at Teschen, Poland. Fortunately he survived the war and by April 1945 was reported as being no longer a PoW.

Private William Cowhoun (44) was also a member of the AMPC when he was reported missing. Like his comrade he was later confirmed as being a PoW. He was moved to Stalag 344 at Lamsdorf, Poland, and survived the war being recorded as no longer a PoW in July 1945.

LESS SOAP USED . . . MORE RESULTS
WHEN YOU ADD CARBOSIL

It's nothing short of magic—that's what women say about Carbosil.
Really, the results obtained with Carbosil are truly amazing. Added
to the water first, it makes your soap extra active. It gives extra
energy to the lather. In short, Carbosil makes your soap work with
all its power—and you use *less* soap to do the work.

**IT'S THE SPECIAL INGREDIENT
IN CARBOSIL THAT TELLS!**

Of course, Carbosil is far and
away the best water softener you
can use. But that's only stage one
of its job. There's a special ingredient in Carbosil which leaps
into action the instant it enters
the water. It removes all objectionable lime hardness—prepares
the water so that soap lathers to
its utmost limit, but without a
bubble wasted. That's how Carbosil
makes your soap extra active.
You get more cleaning value
from it!

**IT'S WHAT CARBOSIL DOES
THAT TELLS, TOO!**

It's astonishing the difference Carbosil makes to washing and cleaning jobs. They are easier—to put
it modestly! And what results!
White washing that's whiter still.
Washing-up that shines because
it's grease-free. Windows that
sparkle with *real* cleanliness.

YET CARBOSIL IS SO MILD!
There's nothing strong or harmful
in Carbosil. Yet it works with such
power. So why not call in Carbosil
now? There's active help for you
in every packet.

Always add a little
CARBOSIL

In big
1d & 2d
packets

FOR WASHING CLOTHES, WASHING UP,
HOUSE CLEANING, WASHING WINDOWS

CAR 174-782

Advert for Carbosil water softener (Sunderland Echo)

Driver Ronald Marlee (21) was serving with the Royal Army Service Corps (RASC) when he too was taken prisoner during the fall of France. His family at Crosslea Avenue received news in September that he had become a PoW and it was later confirmed that he was being detained at Stalag 344 at Lamsdorf, Poland. Once again, he survived the war and by late August 1945 was reported as no longer being a PoW.

Private Matthew Holland, 6th Battalion, DLI, was also captured in France and was later incarcerated at Stalag 20b at Marienburg in Poland. Private Holland (21), whose home was at Roker Park Road South, also survived the war and is listed as no longer being a PoW in mid-June 1945.

Lance Corporal Frank Young of Elemore Lane was serving with the 11th DLI when he was taken prisoner in May. His family faced an anxious wait until late August before it was confirmed that he was indeed a PoW. He was later located at Stalag 4c at Wistritz Bei Teplitz in Czechoslovakia. Once again, he survived the war and by late June was no longer a PoW. One question regarding Frank was that of his rank, as most documents refer to him as a lance corporal but newspaper accounts and some documents from 1946 refer to him as a private.

Private William Howe (20) from Front Street, Old Penshaw, was also serving with the 11th DLI when he was reported missing following the fall of France. He was listed as a PoW in September and was held, like his comrade above, at Wistritz Bei Teplitz. He too survived the war ad was listed as no longer being a PoW in late July.

Private John Parkin (23) was taken prisoner in France while serving with the Black Watch (Royal Highlanders) (1st Tyneside Scottish). At a later date, Private Parkin was also reportedly being held at Stalag 344 at Lamsdorf. In December 1940, it was announced that the young soldier, who lived at Zetland Street, had been awarded the Military Medal (MM). Private Parkin survived his time in captivity and in mid-June was described as no longer being a prisoner of the Germans.

Sapper Robert H. Mason (23) of Rainton Street, Seaham, was serving with 1 Field Squadron, Royal Engineers, when he was captured and his family had to wait until late October before he was confirmed as a PoW being held at Stalag 20b at Marienburg, Poland. Once again, there was a happy ending as he survived the war and was listed as no longer being a prisoner in late August 1945.

Gunner Norman Anderson was taken prisoner, aged just 20, while he was serving in France with the 1st Battery, 1st Searchlight Regiment, Royal Artillery. Captured on 26 May he spent time in four PoW camps during his time as a prisoner. Gunner Anderson lived at the Parade, Hendon, and had worked as a labourer before the war and had joined the army in October 1939. He survived his ordeal as a PoW.

Gunner Charles Reynolds (21) was captured while serving with the 2/1 Searchlight Regiment, Royal Artillery, when he too was captured. Initially posted missing he was confirmed as a PoW in early August and was held at Stalag 20a at Thorn Podgorz in Poland until August 1945 when he was listed as no longer being a PoW.

Trooper William Madgin was aged 20 when he was captured while serving with the 1st Lothian & Borders Horse, Royal Armoured Corps. Initially reported missing on 19 July 1940 he was confirmed as having been taken prisoner in early August. For young William, however, there would be no happy ending. He is listed as having been repatriated in late September 1944 as he was presumable either in ill health or was suffering from wounds and he succumbed on 3 February 1945. Trooper Madgin was not a Sunderland man. He had been born at Staveley, Derbyshire, but appears to have lived in Sunderland before the war. He was the only son of Lydia and the late Nicholas Madgin and lies in St Helen's Cemetery in Lancashire.

Late on the night of 9 August, there were a small number of enemy bombers active over the north-east and at approximately 11.40pm a Heinkel He 111, which had been attacked and badly damaged by RAF fighters, jettisoned its bomb load as it attempted to make it home. Unfortunately, the bomber was over Sunderland at the time and the bombs fell on the shipyard of Sir James Laing & Sons Ltd., a nearby railway bridge, several houses

L/Cpl. Thomas Davison (39), A.M.P.C., High Street East, Sunderland (missing).

Dvr. Ronald Marlee (24), R.A.S.C., Crosslea Avenue, Sunderland (missing).

Pte. William Cowhoun (47), A.M.P.C., Wall Street, Sunderland (missing).

Pte. Frank Young, Elemore Lane, Easington Lane (missing).

Spr. Robert H. Mason (23), R.E., Rainton Street, Seaham (missing).

Gnr. Charles Reynolds (21), R.A., High Dubmire, Fence Houses (prisoner).

Tpr. William Madgin (20), Lothian and Border Yeomanry, late of Sunderland (missing).

Pte. William Howe (20), D.L.I., Front Street, Old Penshaw (missing).

Sunderland men taken prisoner of war during the fall of France (Sunderland Echo)

and the Monkwearmouth Station Hotel. Four civilians lost their lives in the attack. The youngest to lose his life was 18-year-old Thompson Reed of 27 Washington Street, Millfield. A member of the Air Training Corps (ATC) Mr Reed was injured and later died at Sunderland Royal Infirmary. Miss Irene Mooney (19) lived at 86 Maplewood Avenue, Monkwearmouth, and was reportedly injured in Monkwearmouth (unconfirmed reports have her as near to the Laing's yard) and died four days later at Monkwearmouth and Southwick Hospital. The remaining victims were killed at Laing's. Richard Archer (33) was a married man and left behind his widow, Jesstina Holm Archer, at the couples' home at 15 Miller Street and his father, Robert, at 26 Wear Street. Mr Archer was injured in the bombing and died the same day at the Sunderland Royal Infirmary. Mr Arthur Perry (26) was the son of Walter and Catherine Perry of 37 Henderson Road, he was killed instantly. The He 111 that had dropped the bombs crashed into the North Sea shortly afterwards with the four-man crew being taken prisoner.

On the night of 12 August bombs once more fell on Sunderland and its immediate hinterlands. One of these bombs resulted in the death of the first Home Guard in the area to lose his life through enemy action. Thirty-year-old Andrew Smith Errington lived at 16 Seaton Crescent, Seaton Lane, Seaham, with his wife Alice Maud Errington. He also left behind his father, also named Andrew Smith Errington, at 21 Rutland Street, Seaham. The Home Guardsman died from his injuries on 13 August at Sunderland Royal Infirmary.

With the Battle of Britain continuing to rage, the men of Bomber Command found themselves launched against a variety of targets, ranging from the invasion ports to industrial targets in Germany. On the night of 16/17 August, the Command dispatched 102 aircraft to 5 targets in Germany and to airfields in Belgium, France and Holland. Amongst those taking part were the Handley Page Hampdens of 144 Squadron. Two of its aircraft, which were sent to Merseburg, failed to return on this night. Among the six of the aircrew to lose their lives on this night was another Sunderland man. Sergeant Robert Leslie Wake (28) was the observer aboard Hampden I (P4291). Both Sergeant Wake and one of the crew's wireless operator/air gunners were killed and buried at the Reichswald Forest War Cemetery. Another two of the crew escaped and were captured and taken prisoner. Sergeant Wake was the son of Robert Finlay Wake and Pamala Wake.

In the early hours of 26 August, enemy aircraft were once again active over the north-east and, despite the activity of the anti-aircraft units around Sunderland, a single bomb fell onto the area of Marina Avenue resulting in seven people being injured. The next few days followed a similar pattern of enemy aircraft being active but although there was a minor raid on Sunderland on the night of 31 August there was little or no damage and only a few minor injuries.

Late on 5 September and into the early hours of 6 September, the Germans once again raided the north-east. At 11.18pm, an enemy bomber crossed the coast but was immediately picked up by searchlights and engaged by the anti-aircraft battery at Ryhope Road, Grangetown. A direct hit was scored on the bomber and the tail was blown off and caught fire. The aircraft, a Heinkel He 111, crashed onto Suffolk Street, killing one resident, Rachel Stormont (41) at no. 55½ and trapping a family in a surface air raid shelter. The bodies of two of the crew, Obergefreiter Rudolf Marten (wireless operator) and Gefreiter Josef Wich (mechanic) were discovered in the wreckage but the two others were found dead, having either been thrown clear or having attempted to bail out of the stricken aircraft. They were Oberleutnant Hans W. Schroder (pilot), whose terribly injured body was found in the garden of 5 Grange Crescent with his unopened parachute, and Unteroffizier Franz Reitz, who was found dead on top of an air raid shelter at Bede Towers. His parachute had opened but he too had suffered terrible injuries. The four Luftwaffe airmen

Damage on Suffolk Street. Military officers inspect the remains of the crashed German bomber (Sunderland Echo)

were buried at Hylton Cemetery, where they remain to this day. The fire from the crashed bomber attracted further aircraft, and in the early hours two bombs demolished Central Station and several nearby properties.

Bomb damage at Central Station (Sunderland Public Libraries)

Damage to Joseph & Son's toyshop on Union Street after wreckage from Central Station was blown into the shop (Sunderland Public Libraries)

Sporadic and usually small-scale raids continued on Sunderland throughout the rest of the year with the Germans switching to night attacks after their bombers received a severe mauling at the hands of RAF Fighter Command off the north-east coast in mid-September. During these small raids there was a steady drip effect of both casualties and damage to property, although little serious damage was done to important industrial locations.

Although the war news continued to be bleak, many young people, caught up in the drama of the moment, took the decision to get married, especially if one, or both, were in the services. Saturday, 7 September saw the marriage of Sergeant Norman Gilbert Donald, RAF, to Miss Jean Ashdown Williamson. The service took place at St Andrew's Church, Roker, and both young people were Sunderland residents with Sergeant Donald (23) being the eldest son of Mrs and Mrs Norman and Dorothy Donald of 8 Marcia Avenue and Miss Williamson the daughter of Mr and Mrs Fred Williamson of 11 Gillside Grove, Roker. The bridesmaids were Misses Edna Gray, Constance Holmes (both cousins of the bride), and Audrey Clifford, while the best man was Mr Arthur Steele. Sergeant Donald had just qualified as a compositor with the *Sunderland Echo* at the outbreak of war and had immediately joined the RAF. Like many a wartime marriage the couple did not set up home together at first, as Sergeant Donald was preparing to go abroad for pilot training and so the new Mrs Donald instead continued to live at her parents' home.

In September, the success of Joseph L. Thompson & Sons Ltd. in constructing 'Empire' type tramps had convinced the British government to send a delegation to the United States to advise the US Maritime Commission on the construction of the type. The two senior members of this delegation were Cyril Thompson, managing director of the yard, and Harry Hunter of the North Eastern Marine Engineering Co. Ltd. of Wallsend and Sunderland. The main part of their visit was a tour of the yards of Henry Kaiser and resulted in an option for the building of sixty such ships (which the Americans named the 'Ocean' type), being taken. Cyril Thompson was returning to Britain aboard the motor passenger ship *Western Prince,* when shortly before 9.00am on the morning of 14 September the unescorted ship was torpedoed and sunk by U-96. All but 15 of the 168 passengers and crew aboard took to the boats but it was to be 9 hours before Mr Thompson and the other survivors were rescued by the SS *Baron Kinnaird* and HMS *Active.* Mr Thompson continued to the USA by air and the contract for the sixty ships was signed on 20 December.

October brought the case of the murder of 78-year-old widow, Emma Jane Harrison, before Durham Assizes. The prosecutor, Mr Paley Scott, KC, told the court that the case was a sordid and miserable one in which drink had played a very large part. It was explained how 19-year-old Sapper John Charles Mather had returned home on a short leave and had told his mother that he only had 1*s* to his name. His mother and grandmother had therefore borrowed 2*s* from neighbours to spend on drink. His mother had also pawned blankets to raise further funds for what turned into a pub crawl around the town. Mather's grandmother, Mrs Pallas, had also borrowed from neighbours,

The Western Prince, *which was carrying Mr Thompson (Unknown)*

including a contribution of 2s 6d from Mrs Harrison, who lived in the same building. At around 9.00pm, the trio had returned to Mrs Pallas' room and, as referred to previously, Mather had gone to borrow a further sum from Mrs Harrison. After his return, the trio had visited more public houses until closing time.

Confessing to his crime, Mather had stated that he had borrowed 10s from Mrs Harrison and when she had asked what he wanted the money for he had told her it was to buy a gill. Upon hearing this, the widow had cast doubt on his mother's character causing him to lose his temper and strike her on the head with a coal rake. Upon arriving at Mrs Harrison's home the police had found the room locked but were able to unlock the door using a key found in the possession of the accused. Inside, they had found the body of the elderly lady, a bloodied coal rake and two broken knives. When Mather had presented himself at the police station to confess, his clothes had been bloodstained. Medical evidence presented to the court included evidence that Mrs Harrison had suffered severe head trauma with 'five terrible wounds on the head, three of which smashed the skull'.

Mather, who had been married before he was aged 17 and had previously been of good character, could only offer in defence that he had been drink-taken and had no intent to commit the awful crime to which had confessed. The prosecution, however, said that for drunkenness to be used as a defence for altering the charge from murder to manslaughter a man would have had to be so drunk that he was incapable of forming an intent to cause any harm at all, in other words, 'he would have to reduce himself almost to a condition of a raving lunatic'. If Mather had been in such a state, the prosecution avowed, he would have been incapable of remembering the crime or describing the murder weapon to police the next morning. The prosecution alleged that the real intent of the crime was the desire to obtain more money to continue the drinking spree on which the family had embarked. Mr Paley Scott, prosecuting, did, however, tell the jury that although they must have some sympathy for Mather they must also balance this with the knowledge that his mother was morally much to blame for the tragic events of the night.

Under cross-examination, Mrs Mather admitted that she was a heavy drinker and, although she claimed to have lessened her drinking recently, had to admit that up until June she had commonly been observed to have consumed, on a daily basis, up to ten pints of beer before 8.00pm.

One witness, Mrs Cokley, stated that on the night in question she had been visited by Mather and his mother. They had invited her for a drink but she had declined and testified that the young soldier was clearly drunk. She went on to describe how his 'eyes were dazzling and he could hardly get his words out'. She told the court that she had told him she was sorry to see him in such a state and that up until that time she 'never knew the boy to take drink before', adding, 'He had been a fine boy'.[23] It also emerged that Mrs Harrison had a reputation locally as an unregistered moneylender.

The jury did clearly have some sympathy for Mather and returned a not guilty verdict to the charge of murder but found the young soldier guilty of manslaughter. Sentencing him to seven years' penal servitude, Mr Justice Cassells said that in his drunken condition he had attacked an old woman and beaten her to death. Continuing, he said that Mather had been fortunate that the jury had 'taken a merciful view of the circumstances'. Summing up, Mr Cassells said that the jury had clearly been swayed by the opinion that much of the blame, at least morally, fell upon Mather's mother and that their duty had been a difficult one on which they had to try 'a young man who may well be paying the penalty not only of his own folly, but his mother's'. He hoped that she would 'not be happy when she saw the results of her handiwork'. Concluding, he added that it was 'indeed, a sordid story'.[24]

With the war now at the forefront of all minds, it should come as no surprise that the annual poppy appeal was more successful than ever in 1940. In December, the Sunderland branch of the British Legion announced that the appeal had raised the record sum of £914 9s 8d compared with £819 17s in 1939.

With the weather turning cold as winter went on and, in the spirit of wartime Britain, the local press offered a variety of tips on how to stay warm without using extra supplies or unobtainable items. One of these tips, presented in the *Sunderland Echo* of 4 December, was to sew a yard-wide length of cretonne to the edges of an eiderdown and tuck it under the mattress when making the bed. This, it was claimed, would keep the eiderdown in place no matter how restless the sleeper was and was especially useful for the beds of children and for cots.

By mid-December, the Board of Education had agreed to pay for 100 per cent of the costs of erecting air raid shelters at schools. The only proviso was that the grants could only be paid on contracts placed on or after 19 October 1940. This meant that Sunderland would lose out in the sum of approximately £40,000 simply because it had been ahead of the game in organising shelters for the schools in its area. The rules just introduced meant that the town could only apply retrospectively for grants to cover 50 per cent of the costs.

With the approach of the second wartime Christmas, many people in Sunderland turned their thoughts to loved ones, or even strangers, who were serving elsewhere in the forces. Many organisations banded together to provide Christmas comfort packages for service personnel. Foremost amongst them was the WVS. Throughout November and December the volunteers collated and sorted parcels for servicemen before organising their postage. The volunteers ranged from unassuming housewives to the mayoress. The majority of parcels contained a variety of items, the format of which had been thought out in advance. They contained items such as cigarettes, handkerchiefs, chocolate, combs, shaving sticks, razors, soap, toothpaste and dental cream. Throughout the build-up to the festive season, the WVS advertised widely for donations for the comfort fund, both in terms of items for parcels and money to cover postage. Local churches were also active in providing Christmas comfort parcels for those of their congregation who were serving.

There were also a large number of servicemen and women based in Sunderland itself and the authorities were keen to ensure that they enjoyed the Christmas season in the town. Many events, both large and small, were organised. One of the largest and grandest events was a dance for 1,000 service personnel arranged by the Wearside Council for Coordination of Welfare Work.

There were also large numbers of seamen present in Sunderland and the Sunderland Mission to Seamen put together a large and varied programme of events to entertain these men. One of the greatest problems facing the mission staff was securing enough food to provide some semblance of a traditional Christmas meal to the seamen based in the area. An appeal was made to the public, and women especially, of Wearside to donate to the cause, whether in money or food.

With the postal service expecting a surge in business, the people of Sunderland were warned to post their Christmas cards and parcels earlier than normal and, in the main, they complied with this instruction. By 19 December the postal service was reporting that fewer cards had been sent this year but there had been a large increase in the number of parcels. The biggest increase was in the number of registered parcels and letters, a very large proportion of which were being sent to men and women in the forces. In order to cope with demand, the post office in Sunderland had taken on almost double the number of temporary staff with some 269 men and women being employed in this capacity. Eighty or ninety of these temporary workers were women, with approximately half being employed directly on deliveries. The usual Christmas Eve rush to post last-minute items was simply non-existent at Sunderland and the Post Office and its staff expressed their gratitude to the public for heeding the warnings to post early.

The strict regulations which had been introduced to prevent people from entering areas which were militarily important had already resulted in a number of prosecutions, the majority of them caused through ignorance or misunderstandings. Late December saw another such case, one which stirred the sympathy of the magistrates. Dutch seaman Jacobus Roos (20) had been employed on the Wear but had been moved to the Tyne. During his time on Wearside he had met a young woman and the two had begun courting. In mid-December he had visited Sunderland but the police were called after he tried to pay for a hotel room and it was discovered that his Dutch passport was not stamped with the necessary permissions for him to enter Sunderland. Detective Turnock stated that he had questioned Roos who had told him that one of the officers on his ship had told him it would be perfectly acceptable for him to travel to Sunderland. When the magistrates asked Roos why he had come to Sunderland he told them that it was solely to see his girlfriend. The chairman, Mr Fred Williamson, asked Superintendent Smith how it might be possible for Roos to visit Sunderland without breaking the law and was informed that the only way was for him to obtain permission from Sunderland police and that it would be easier for his girlfriend to travel to Tyneside. Mr Roos told the court that this was impossible, and it was agreed that in future he should inform Newcastle police who would in turn inform their counterparts in Sunderland. Despite having the sympathy of the bench, Roos was still found guilty of contravening the Defence Regulations and fined £1.

Wartime Christmases were stressful for those trying to run a household. The added pressures of rationing, shortages and queuing placed additional strain on many a Sunderland

Cleadon C of E nativity play (Sunderland Echo)

housewife as she tried to ensure that the traditional Christmas celebrations, or as close as possible, could be maintained. For those with children there were added problems as toy production was effectively halted in wartime Britain as factories were turned over to crucial war work. As Christmas approached there were still some aspects of life which were comfortingly normal. Many schools still put on Nativity plays and many proud parents found the time to go and see the plays and to take their minds off the war for a short time.

CHAPTER 3

1941: A Year of Struggle and Heartbreak

As the third year of the war opened, Sunderland was becoming accustomed to air raids and alerts. Several people had already been killed in the town but air raid defences and precautions were strengthening and the perceived victory of the Battle of Britain had boosted morale somewhat. A small raid on 15/16 February caused a sleepless night and some damage in the town, as enemy aircraft ranged over the north-east. On the night of 23 February, a bomb scored a direct hit on 5 Tunstall Vale. Several houses were destroyed and seven people, including a 6-month old baby, were killed in the incident.

People Killed during the Raid on 23 February.

Name	Age	Address
Violet Temple Coward	29	3 Tunstall Vale
Amelia Sharp	63	3 Tunstall Vale
Irene Sharp	27	3 Tunstall Vale
Mary Thompson	76	7 Tunstall Vale
Margaret Armstrong	23	20 Tunstall Vale
Antoinette Sloan	21	20 Tunstall Vale
Joyce Sloan	6 months	20 Tunstall Vale

The night of 9/10 April brought a very heavy attack on the communities at the mouth of the Tyne and fire units from

Bomb damage at no. 7 Tunstall Vale (Sunderland Public Libraries)

Sunderland, along with other areas, responded in answer to pleas for aid. In the early hours, Sunderland itself was hit when two bombs fell on the area of Fawcett Street causing extensive property damage and a fire which gutted the Binns store. Two people, John James Bower (16) and Laura Sinclair (24), were killed at 10 and 11 Ethel Street respectively.

Bomb damage at Binns, Fawcett Street (Sunderland Public Libraries)

Five nights later, the Luftwaffe returned with a raid scattered over the north-east, including Sunderland. Between 1.50am and 4.40am, bombs dropped at several locations in the town, causing significant property damage. Included amongst the premises damaged were those of Sunderland Forge & Engineering Co. (where several people were killed) and T.W. Greenwell & Co. at South Dock. Parachute mines and bombs also destroyed or severely damaged the Victoria Hall, the Palatine Hotel, the Winter Gardens, Mowbray Park and the museum and art gallery. In total eighteen people were killed, thirty-six seriously injured and seventy-nine slightly injured.

On 2 June, Joseph Robert Kayll, DSO, DFC, returned to the fray as wing commander at RAF Hornchurch. On 25 July, Kayll was part of a flight of three Spitfires being led by the station commander, Group Captain Harry Broadhurst, when they were bounced by a superior force of ME109s. Only Broadhurst was not shot down. Wing Commander Kayll crash-landed his stricken Spitfire near St Omer and was captured almost

The Victoria Hall, wrecked by a parachute mine which also severely damaged the Winter Gardens (Sunderland Public Libraries)

Wing Commander Kayll (Unknown)

immediately. After being interrogated, where the Germans revealed that they knew a great deal about him from various sources including the *Sunderland Echo*, he was sent to Oflag IX (A/H) at Spangenburg Castle. Here, he helped to orchestrate several escape attempts and in October he was moved to Stalag VI Bad Wartburg.

Visits to Wearside from various dignitaries and celebrities were fairly commonplace during the war, as they were seen as being a good way to boost morale and to make sure that the people of the area felt their involvement in the war effort was valued. On 19 June, the king and queen arrived without any warning (a security measure as it was necessary to restrict knowledge of the movements and whereabouts of the royal couple throughout the war for obvious reasons). Beginning their tour at a large shipyard, the news of the royal couple's presence 'flashed round Sunderland and the main streets were thronged with people as the king and queen drove to the station to entrain for Teesside'. The visit was part of a two-day long tour of war industries in the north-east. The visit, though unannounced, was not a complete surprise as the royal couple had spent the previous day touring the Armstrong's facilities on Tyneside and on the morning of the visit to Wearside, they had visited a munitions factory in County Durham.

Upon arrival at Sunderland the king and queen were greeted by the mayor, Councillor Myers Wayman, and Chief Constable G.H. Cook. At this stage the royal couple were accompanied by Sir Arthur Lambert, the Civil Defence Commissioner for the Northern Region, and Admiral Wellwood Maxwood. For the visit the king was wearing the undress uniform of Admiral of the Fleet while the queen was attired in a two-piece ensemble in a mushroom shade, with a matching felt hat.

On the journey to the riverside, the visitors were cheered by crowds lining the route. At Hylton Road Schools, the children had been assembled in the playground and cheered excitedly as the royal couple waved happily to them as they passed by.

Upon arriving at the shipyard, the royal visitors were given an enthusiastic welcome, which caused one reporter to comment that their majesties had remarked to him that: 'Sunderland folk certainly know how to give a welcome. I give them top marks for enthusiasm.'[25] The visit had been timed to coincide with the lunch hour and, therefore, the shipyard was not as noisy as usual for the visit, which was marked by a friendly informality. Reporters told how the visit was like a royal garden party attended by men in oil-stained dungarees rather than frock coats and instead of beautiful gardens the backdrop was one of the hulls of merchant ships. Their majesties walked amongst the groups of men who were sitting in the yard eating their lunch. As they did so they talked with groups of workers about a variety of topics related to their work. In particular, two apprentice fitter and turners, Thomas Lawton of Enfield Street and Ralph Haswell of Westmoor Road (both aged 15), were picked out by the visitors. The queen asked how long the boys had worked in the shipyard and whether they enjoyed their jobs. Responding without any shyness the two apprentices told the queen, 'It's grand being here.' Another worker, though at the opposite end of the age spectrum, who enjoyed a few moments of conversation with the royal couple was John Walker (74) who was introduced to the king and queen informally with, 'This is Johnny Walker. Like his famous namesake, he's still going strong, although he's been here sixty years.' Although the ageing worker continued to chew gum throughout his interview, his answers caused the king to laugh heartily.

Several of the members of the yards' Home Guard unit were on duty in dungarees at the time of the visit and their majesties picked out John Haswell of Lyndhurst Terrace to converse with. After being asked by the queen if he had served in the last war, he informed her that he had joined the army but had been recalled to work in the shipyard before being sent overseas.

Many of the workers were anxious to meet the visitors and on one occasion the royal couple were surrounded by a throng of workers and for several minutes there was 'a continuous round of good-humoured banter'. Relating some of the conversation to a reporter afterwards, foreman-plater Harry Gibson of Henderson Place said how, at one stage, the queen had been speaking to a diminutive 'catcher' boy who, like most of the boys, was wearing a set of overalls that were too large for him and one of the men remarked that there was plenty of room for him to grow into. The queen laughed at the remark before observing that now that clothing was rationed it would be more necessary than ever for boys to inherit their fathers' old suits. The king had told Mr Gibson that it looked as though everyone was pulling together and Mr Gibson had replied that that was the intention of everyone in the yard. Certainly, the attitude of the workers in the yard could not be faulted and, as their majesties walked between lines of shipyard workers and workers from neighbouring concerns, two workmen held up a blackboard on which had been chalked the message: 'We will whack 'em, nothing surer, Fatty Goering and his Fuhrer.'[26] Upon seeing the

The King and Queen Visit a Sunderland Shipyard in June 1941 (Sunderland Echo)

message, the queen smiled. At the conclusion of their visit, the royal couple inspected two large ships which were being fitted out, showing great interest in the accommodation provided for the crew before spending several minutes looking at the engine room.

At the railway station, a considerable crowd had gathered to see the royal visitors off. On the platform, dignitaries, including the mayor and the town clerk (Mr G.S. McIntire), led the cheering as the royal party departed. Speaking afterwards to the *Sunderland Echo,* the mayor told the newspaper that their majesties had long memories and remembered clearly their last visit to Sunderland which had taken place in 1939. The queen had particularly remembered the guard of honour which had been formed by 'the sailor boys' of the Sunderland Boys' Orphanage. The king, meanwhile, remembered placing the final rivet in the new Wearmouth Bridge.

The day after the royal visit, another Sunderland firm fell victim to the strict food regulations. Gallons Ltd. was fined the sum of 10s for selling rationed food (cooking fats) to persons who were not registered with the firm. The incident involved the firm's branch on Dundas Street and revolved around a household of four persons who were registered at the shop for bacon, sugar and butter but not for cooking fats. It had been determined in May that Gallons had been supplying this household with cooking fats and when approached, the manageress had explained that this had been an oversight on the part of the staff. It was accepted that there was no ulterior motive behind the offence and that it had been an honest mistake resulting, partially, from the lack of re-registration in January. Nevertheless, the firm was still fined.

Although most of the crimes heard were of a relatively minor sort such as that above, there was serious concern over the rising levels of juvenile crime in the Sunderland area at the time. One case involved five boys aged 7–13 who were accused and found guilty of wilfully damaging an air raid shelter in Hylton Road playing field. The boys had been caught by the caretaker of the field and he had smacked at least one of the boys on the face. The boy's father later caused a scene in Faraday Grove where he threatened to shoot the caretaker, Mr Henry Mallam, or to cause him to lose his job, claiming that his son had returned home badly bruised about his entire body from a beating administered by Mr Mallam. Fining the parents of the children 10s apiece and ordering each to pay damages of 8s each the chairman, Mr F. Williamson, remarked that if he had caught the boys they certainly would have been 'black and blue from head to foot. I cannot blame him for smacking their faces.'[27]

Other juvenile crime was encouraged by the potential profits to be made from the resale of food and there had been a rash of thefts from allotments, gardens and orchards. Testifying at Sunderland Juvenile Court in the prosecution of a 13-year-old boy accused of causing £3 of damage to allotment owned by a Mr George Evans of Chester Road, Chief Detective Inspector Middlemist stated that: 'This type of offence is becoming very frequent, and I would ask the public to be very suspicious of young boys who come round the streets hawking lettuce and other similar things.' Mr Evans, who was an ex-serviceman, testified that he had suffered the theft, or loss through damage, of 350 heads of lettuce in the last few days. On one occasion Mr Evans had managed to apprehend the 13-year-old lad who had seventy lettuces in a wheelbarrow. The boy had told him that he had got the lettuces from the school garden but at the police station had given a false name and address. Apprehended later, the boy had confessed to stealing the lettuces from the property of Mr Evans and that he had sold lettuces from a previous theft for 3s. The chairman, Mr Williamson, once more placed the boy on probation for two years, ordered his father to repay Mr Evans the sum of £3 at a rate of 10s per week and bound him over for the sum of £5. Mr Williamson commented that he would have ordered the lad to be birched but that this would have prevented him from ordering the repayment for the damage caused.

The first day of July brought tragedy as a 12-year-old Sunderland boy, James David Browell, lost his life as a result of some youthful misadventure. The youngster had illegally entered a prohibited area along with three of his friends. Upon gaining entry, disregarding several warning signs, the foursome had found an object lying on the ground and began throwing it to one another. One of the boys then threw the object onto a rock where it exploded. Three of the boys, William Hugh Beatty (11) of 9 Short Street, Henley, George Lennox (12), and his brother Alexander (11), both of 13 Ward Street, Hendon, were injured, while Browell was killed. As the three injured boys lay helpless, two RAF men, Corporal H. Smith and Aircraftman J. Atkinson entered the area despite the risk to themselves and helped to rescue the surviving boys. At the inquest the coroner told the two men that he would make sure that their actions on that night were reported to their superiors and that their 'action was worthy of the highest praise'.[28]

Tragedy once again struck on 27 September when merchant seaman Edward Johnson Scott Willey (58) died in the Royal Infirmary. Mr Willey was the second engineering officer aboard the SS *Cormount* and had returned to his home at 2 Colchester Terrace to recover from a recent incident when his ship had been attacked from the air. After taking ill, Mr Willey was treated in hospital but succumbed two days after his admission. At the subsequent inquest his widow, Mrs Bertha Willey, testified that her husband had always been a fit and active man but in her opinion was suffering from shock as a result of his experience. Dr D.A. Heffernan of the Royal Infirmary, however, testified that in his medical opinion there had been no link between Mr Willey's death and his experience at sea and that he had died of kidney disease.[29]

In November there was another raid when a force of medium bombers accompanied by a small number of dive-bombers attacked the Tyne-Tees area on 7/8 November. In Sunderland there was damage to the LNER railway and a quay at South Docks when bombs fell on the area. One engine was on the line when a bomb detonated just in front of it, blowing the engine off the rails and leaving it turned at a right angle to the lines. Rail transport was disrupted by both damage and by the presence of an unexploded bomb. Property damage was extensive with many people bombed out of their homes, and a rest centre was opened to cope with over 100 homeless people. A total of seven people were killed in the attack.

Casualties from Attack on 7/8 November 1941.

Name	Age	Location	Notes
John Barras	70	Tyzacks Works, Fulwell Rd	
Joseph Cairns	26	Roker Av	
Joseph Gowland	46	108 Fulwell Rd	
Edwin Smith	8	1 Whitehouse Cott, Hendon	

Madeline Louise Smith	17	1 Whitehouse Cott, Hendon	Fireguard
Madeline Louise Smith	48	1 Whitehouse Cott, Hendon	Fireguard
William E. N. L. Steel	74	8 Lily Street	

Damage to rail lines at South Docks. The engine which had the lucky escape is in the right (Sunderland Public Libraries)

CHAPTER 4

1942: The Tide Turns

❖❖❖

Throughout January, the people of Sunderland were urged to gather and deliver waste paper as part of a national campaign. The people of the town responded in magnificent fashion with schools being particularly eager to contribute to the campaign, organising teams of salvage monitors to sort and stack the paper. At Hudson Street, the school boasted that they had already collected enough paper and cardboard to fill a freighter by 18 January. By the time the campaign had ended, Councillor George Willis, chairman of Sunderland Cleansing Committee, could tell the people of the town that they had done exceptionally well and, although a final count had not yet been made, it was believed that the final tally would be well in excess of 300 tons. He heaped praise on the local schools, telling readers of the local newspaper that on the final day schools had donated 7½ tons of paper and cardboard.

While the people of Sunderland collected waste paper for the war effort others received welcome news of loved ones who had been taken prisoner earlier in the war. In January, pictures of several Sunderland men who were being held at Stalag II.D at Stargard in Poland were published in the local press. On 17 January, the families of Private Thomas Field of 39 Balmoral Terrace, Grangetown, Private Donald Campbell, Northumberland Hussars, of 221 Fulwell Road, and Sergeant Stanley Hunter, of 69 St Leonard Street, must have felt some

Salvage monitors sort paper at Hudson Street School (Sunderland Echo)

relief in seeing the pictures of their loved ones alongside comrades and apparently in good health.

The final day of January brought the death of another Sunderland sailor. Ordinary Seaman Wilfred Nutter (24) was serving aboard the destroyer HMS *Belmont* when she was torpedoed and sank with all hands off the coast of Newfoundland. The *Belmont* had begun life as the US navy destroyer USS *Satterlee* in 1919 but had been placed in reserve in 1922 until being reactivated at the outbreak of the Second World War and transferred to the RN for use as a convoy escort

Sunderland PoWs. Pvt Thomas Field (1), Pvt Donald Campbell (2), and Sergeant Stanley Hunter (3) (Sunderland Echo)

during the Battle of the Atlantic. At the time of her sinking, the *Belmont* had been escorting Convoy NA.2 which consisted of ships ferrying British and Canadian airmen to serve in Britain. Ordinary Seaman Wilfred Nutter lived in Shiney Row with his parents, James and Mary.

HMS Belmont, *seen here as the USS* Satterlee *(Public Domain)*

Ordinary Seaman Wilfred Nutter (Sunderland Echo)

In early February, the destroyer HMS *Worcester* was practising torpedo attacks with the 21st Destroyer Flotilla when, on 12 February, the flotilla was notified of the attempt by the German battlecruisers *Scharnhorst* and *Gneisenau*, along with the heavy cruiser *Prinz Eugen*, to reach a German port after leaving Brest. The 21st Flotilla was ordered to make torpedo attacks on the German ships and during this unsuccessful attempt HMS *Worcester* was badly hit by 11in shells from the battlecruisers and 8in shells from the *Prinz Eugen*. This resulted in the deaths of twenty-six of her crew with another forty-five being injured. There was severe structural damage, including fires and the flooding of the No.1 Boiler Room, and the destroyer was made dead in the water. Her crew managed to repair her enough to set off once more and reached harbour at Harwich where the majority of the dead were buried side-by-side.

One of those who was not buried alongside his shipmates was Leading Seaman Thomas Walshaw (22). Leading Seaman Walshaw lived with his family at 13 Burleigh Garth (they had previously lived at Brougham Street) and his grieving parents, Thomas and Florence, siblings and brother-in-law placed a memorial in the Roll of Honour section of the local press in the days following his death. This was despite the fact that Leading Seaman Walshaw was not confirmed as having been killed but had been declared missing believed killed (it is possible that he had been blown overboard during the attack). A memorial service was held for Walshaw at the Emmanuel Free Church on Hudson Road on Sunday, 22 February. Thomas Walshaw was clearly well regarded by his crewmates, as two of them, George Cockerill and Tommy Housefield, paid tribute to their pal by placing their own commemoration notice in the local press.[30]

Another Sunderland family received better news when it was reported that Fusilier F.D. Elsom (30) had been confirmed as being a prisoner of war in Italy. Fusilier Elsom had initially been reported as being missing in action and his family at 24 Thompson Road had no doubt been anxiously waiting for further news of the soldier. Fusilier Elsom was initially assigned to PoW Camp 85, Tuturano Transit Camp, before being sent to Poland where he was held at Stalag 8b at Teschen. Happily it appears that Fusilier Elsom survived his period of captivity.

The blackout, combined with large numbers of servicemen in the town, could sometimes result in a rise in crime and in mid-February a case of manslaughter, which had arisen as a result of both the blackout and the presence of foreign servicemen, was heard at Durham Assizes. Canadian soldier Angus Mayer (22) of the Royal Engineers had been arrested in mid-December 1941 following an altercation on Union Street, Sunderland. On the night in question, a local shipyard worker, John James MacDonald (51), had been walking with his companion, Mrs Margaret Wardropper, when two soldiers along with two young women bumped into them. Mr MacDonald had remonstrated and, it was alleged, had pushed Mayer – which prompted the Canadian to strike the older man in the face. Mr MacDonald fell and struck his head on the pavement resulting in a fractured skull; he died the next day in hospital. Mayer confessed to the police that he had struck Mr MacDonald, adding that he did not fear the consequences, but had acted in

Leading Seaman Tom Walshaw, killed aboard HMS *Worcester (Sunderland Echo)*

Fusilier F.D. Elsom (Sunderland Echo)

self-defence after he had been pushed, and he had no intention of killing Mr MacDonald. Somewhat surprisingly, the Canadian was acquitted on the charges and released without punishment.

Sunday, 17 May saw a number of parades and events in Sunderland to commemorate the second anniversary of the forming of the Home Guard. In the morning the mayor, Councillor Myers Wayman, and the town clerk, Mr G.S. McIntire, toured the city, inspecting various units and being shown the types of training being undertaken. They were escorted on their tour by the commander of the Sunderland Battalion, Lieutenant Colonel L. Laing and several other officers. The mayor was particularly impressed when a unit of Home Guard marched past wearing respirators. The mayor commented that the men of this unit were very smart and soldierly in their appearance and maintained a fine formation, despite the encumbrance of their respirators. At Smyrna Place, several bombed houses had been made safe and reinforced before being turned over to the Home Guard to practise street-fighting techniques and the mayor and his party watched a demonstration of these techniques as a unit cleared the street of 'enemies' by going house to house and room by room. Moving on to the headquarters of one battle company, the visitors were shown examples of internal administration before a display of bayonet fighting on the Town Moor. At Monkwearmouth Station, another company paraded with automatic weapons and anti-tank weaponry, showing how far the force had moved on from the dark days of 1940. On his final visit of the morning, the mayor was shown around another battle headquarters and inaugurated the new Home Guard pigeon-post communications system by sending a pigeon bearing a message of congratulation to the battalion HQ. The message spoke of the mayor's congratulations to the men of the Home Guard in all they had achieved over the previous two years and concluded by saying that this progress had been 'evidenced by all I have seen today'.

Although the majority of the workforce in the Sunderland area remained firmly behind the war effort, there had been increasing levels of unrest with workers becoming more willing to undertake illegal strike action. Their understanding was that their contribution to the war effort now meant that they had greater bargaining power – despite in most cases having lost the support of national unions due to the TUC policy of assisting the war effort in whatever way was possible.

For the miners, the antipathy towards their employers was long and bitter and old disputes were easily resurrected when wartime guidelines were seen as not being followed. On 4 June, some 5,000 miners and boys walked out from pits at Ryhope, Silksworth and Wearmouth over a pay dispute. The miners alleged that the owners refused to pay the wages guaranteed by the essential works order to twenty-four fillers in the straight south district of the Harvey seam, and on the night of 4 June, the arriving night shift putters refused to descend the shaft and the pit was laid idle. The strike quickly spread to neighbouring pits. At Ryhope, the 2,000 or so men and boys were particularly truculent and voted not to resume work until the matter had been settled in their favour. Workers at Monkwearmouth and Silksworth quickly followed suit. Reflecting wartime attitudes, Durham Miners' Association and the employers refused to enter into negotiations until the men resumed work and there seemed to be little likelihood of discussions beginning. The strike was maintained throughout the next week and a meeting of the miners from Ryhope Colliery held on 10 June resulted in a vote agreeing to remain out until the matter was resolved favourably. The miners at Silksworth, meanwhile, who were disgruntled over the perceived failure of the management to pay a hewer who was doing putter's work for approximately 19s less than what he claimed he was entitled to, agreed to return to work under the condition that the matter was discussed. By the following weekend, the local Industrial Relations Officer had finally got involved at Ryhope and had come to an agreement with the miners that they would resume work, with the guarantee that the complaint would be discussed by the Industrial Relations Officer, the management and representatives of Ryhope Miners' Lodge. The miners at Silksworth were informed that their complaint had been resolved in their favour following an urgent meeting between the Coal Owners' Association and Durham Miners' Association.

The strike revealed a strand of bitterness which ran throughout many County Durham communities and which had only briefly been held in abeyance during the early years of the war. Numerous letters to the local press criticised or defended the striking miners and the tone grew increasingly rancorous, even after the strike had been settled. Responding to a letter from a miner who named himself 'Ryhope Putter' a correspondent to the *Sunderland Echo*, writing under the pseudonym 'Coal Common Sense' said that the argument that they did not wish to strike, put forward by the striking miners, would have been more convincing if the latest strike had not been one of many illegal strikes that had recently taken place in the County Durham coalfield. He went on to say that these strikes had been roundly condemned by the Durham Miners' Association and that the men had ignored the edicts of the association urging them to return to work while the matters were discussed, despite the fact that they themselves elected the local officials. Portraying a lack of patriotism amongst miners, 'Coal Common Sense' concluded by saying that the illegal stoppages resulted in a vital lack of output for the nation.

Responding to the above letter, a woman signing herself 'Miner's Wife' asked if 'Coal Common Sense' and the editors of the paper would like to spend a week filling coals for a combined wage of £4 16s 6d as that is what her husband and his workmate had done on their return to work. She went on to say that the strikes were unavoidable due to the intransigence of the coal owners who, despite being given a fortnight to respond to the miners' demands, had failed to enter into negotiations. In conclusion she stated that only the threat of strikes might guarantee the coal owners agreeing to pay the £5 5s minimum weekly wage.

With the workers of Sunderland's many industrial concerns working longer hours than ever before and the increasing number of women in the workplace, there had been a severe strain placed upon those families with young children. Some firms took measures to provide childcare facilities themselves but at the end of July, Sunderland Health Committee could report that the town's first wartime nursery for the children of war workers would open in August at the refurbished St Mark's Vicarage on Chester Road. The final staff had been appointed with Sister M. L. Lawson of the Hospital for Infectious Diseases being seconded as matron and Miss J. Gowdy as deputy matron.

The committee also heard that the recent outbreak of scabies had shown signs of decreasing. The condition had spread through the crowded working-class parts of the town, where living conditions were conducive to the spread of such ailments and in the week ending 17 July between fifty and sixty cases had been diagnosed. The authorities had undertaken a number of special measures to contain the spread of the condition and the school holidays had also served to restrict its spread. By the following week, the number of cases diagnosed was just twelve.

August brought bad news for the friends and family of Sergeant John Skipsey, of the small village of Haswell Plough. Sergeant Skipsey was an air gunner in 101 Squadron of RAF Bomber Command, based at RAF Stradishall. On the night of 17/18 August, the Command dispatched 139 aircraft to bomb the town of Osnabruck. Although the attack was a success it came at the cost of five aircraft. Amongst them were two from 101 Squadron. Sergeant Skipsey had taken off at 9.45pm as the rear gunner in the crew of Pilot Officer E.H. Brown, RCAF. Nothing more was heard from the Wellington III (*X3654, SR-K*) and the crew were subsequently posted missing.

Although the battle against scabies seemed to be being won there were other problems facing the authorities in the town. In the five weeks ending 25 July, there had been 136 cases of measles diagnosed in comparison to just 99 in the previous 5-week period. In addition to this worrying rise there had been 52 cases of pneumonia, 45 of diphtheria, 14 of scarlet fever and 7 of cerebrospinal fever (meningitis). Efforts to encourage parents to have their children immunised where possible were continuing and were meeting with some success on the town. The numbers having their children immunised against diphtheria were particularly encouraging with 553 children under the age of 5 being immunised in July (up to 25 July), compared with just 223 in June.

The arrest of a Sunderland soldier for the attempted murder of his wife revealed a sorry story of an unhappy marriage affected by sectarianism and poverty. On 22 July, Private Richard Fowler (32) of Ravensworth Street approached a police officer in the street and told him that he had shot his wife at their home. Sergeant Andrew Brunton went to the house and found the soldier's wife, Mrs Alice Rhoda Fowler (26), with a bullet wound to the foot. He also found a service Lee-Enfield rifle with one spent cartridge and three live cartridges loaded. Fowler told the sergeant that he had not meant to shoot his wife and that he had been involved in a dispute with his mother-in-law (who owned and lived in the house) for some time.

A week later the case was heard at Sunderland Police Court and the charge of attempted murder was reduced to one of causing grievous bodily harm. Private Fowler pleaded not guilty and told the court how he had endured a very unhappy married life and had been driven to drink by it. The couple had married in 1934 and had two young children together but they had wed without the permission of Alice's mother and this is where the trouble had begun. The couple did not possess enough money to set up their own home and were forced to live with the disapproving mother-in-law. It seems that Alice's mother had a violent dislike of Roman Catholics and for this reason she despised Private Fowler. Indeed, he informed the court, she had told the couple immediately after their marriage that she would do everything in her power to split them apart; the war and the enforced separation of the couple had given her the opportunity to turn Alice against her husband.

Private Fowler described how he had become increasingly desperate for the couple to set up their own home, away from the influence of his mother-in-law, but Alice had continually refused to leave her mother. Indeed, Private Fowler had even asked a minister to persuade his wife that the best option would be to set up their own home – but to no avail. He went on to describe how he had volunteered for foreign service in order to raise more money to buy or rent a house and that, after his return from Dunkirk, he had found the situation at home even worse, with his wife refusing even to go out with him while he was on leave.

On the night in question, his wife alleged that he had been drinking, had argued with her, and that he had taken his rifle and told her was going to shoot her and the children. She said he had then ejected a cartridge to prove the rifle was loaded before shooting her in the foot. She had struggled with him before fleeing the room.

Private Fowler told a different version of events. He claimed that on the evening of 22 July he had become so fed up with the situation that he told his wife he would return early to his unit rather than remain in the Ravensworth Street home. His wife had disparagingly replied that she did not believe him and, growing desperate, he had taken up his rifle solely with the intention of scaring her into believing he was serious. She had still not believed him so he had ejected a cartridge to prove to her that the rifle was indeed loaded. At this point, he alleged, his wife had grabbed the rifle and the two had struggled causing the rifle to fire, wounding her in the foot. Private Fowler concluded by describing how he had lifted the rifle above his head to get it out of the way of his wife and reiterated that he had intended only to scare her and that he had never lifted his hands to her in all their married life.

The bench obviously felt for Private Fowler but had no option but to find him guilty as charged. The president of the bench, Mr F. Williamson, commented, upon sentencing Private Fowler to prison for three months, that 'The Bench reluctantly find you guilty ... we feel that you have been under very grave provocation, not only on this leave but for some time past and have had a very unhappy home life.'[31]

The Dig for Victory campaign continued to enjoy widespread popularity on Wearside, with many householders replacing flower gardens with crops, taking on allotments or joining pig or poultry clubs. In 1941, the Royal Horticultural Society (RHS) and the Ministry of Agriculture had put on a very successful display of photographs of vegetables at Sunderland Museum. This success was followed in July 1942 with an exhibition which concentrated on the pests that afflicted vegetable gardeners. The exhibition, held in the conveniently titled *Gardeners' Friends and Foes* section of the museum, included depictions and descriptions of pests such as wire worm, cut worm, gall weevil, carrot, cabbage and onion flies, the flea beetle, the millipede and centipede, as well as advice on how to best combat the pests.

Amongst the Sunderland-born entertainers who had been taking part in shows for service personnel was a young actress named Molly Thornton. Miss Thornton, the daughter of a Chester Road bus driver, had been involved in these performances from the very beginning of the war, even though she was just a teenager. By 1942, she was attaining some fame, despite being still only 17. By July, Miss Thornton had performed in over 400

The Sunderland Actress and Sex Symbol, Christine Norden (born Mary Lydia 'Molly' Thornton) (Unknown)

shows for Northern Command Entertainments. Many of the people of Sunderland followed her career with interest and on the morning of Saturday, 18 July her fans were able to listen to her feature in a BBC radio broadcast from Manchester.[32]

With the limited opportunities for entertainment, travel restrictions caused by the rationing of petrol and the public being repeatedly urged to avoid travel, even by train (unless it was absolutely necessary) the Sunderland local authority, as elsewhere, had thrown itself into the Holidays-at-Home campaign. This campaign, which ran in July and August, provided numerous opportunities for leisure pursuits and expanded as the war went on. The 1942 campaign offered a very extensive programme of widely publicised events. In just three days of July (18-20), for example, there was a swimming gala held by various youth organisations at the High Street Baths, the opportunity to tour the gardens of Mr T.R. Sewell at Highcroft, Whitburn, a performance by the Horden Colliery Band at Roker Park, and a garden party held by the church of St Nicholas at Bainbridge Holme.

The museum and art galleries' authorities were also playing a full part in the Holidays-at-Home campaign by ambitiously hosting three exhibitions at the same time. In addition to the gardening exhibitions mentioned previously, there was also a screen display at Sunderland Museum of some of the works of R.G. Eves, the portrait and landscape painter who had died in 1941 at Middleton-in-Teesdale. The main attraction, however, was an RAF exhibition held at the art gallery.

Many of the Holidays-at-Home events also raised money for worthy wartime causes. Amongst these was the fund for comforts for those Sunderland men who had found themselves prisoners of war. Many of these men had been taken prisoner in 1940 during the fall of France and the local press continued to feature photographs and news of many of these men, reminding the people of the town of the sacrifices that had already been made and were continuing to be made by men and women of the town. On 30 July, for example, the *Sunderland Echo* featured a photograph of Private Frank Docherty of Carlyon Street, as a PoW at Stalag XXA, sandwiched between accounts of Holidays-at-Home activities and an advert for the ongoing 'Tanks for Attack' campaign.

The government 'Tanks for Attack' campaign ran between July and September, with local communities being urged to contribute towards the campaign to buy more tanks for the British army. Part of the campaign was the drive to encourage small savers to redouble their efforts. Fostering a competitive atmosphere, communities were informed that those which reached or surpassed an increase of 20 per cent of small savings compared to the previous year would be granted the privilege of having the name of their town or district painted onto the tank which they had paid for. An increase of 20 per cent would purchase a light tank, 25 per cent a medium tank and 30 per cent a heavy tank. Communities were also told that alongside the name of their town or district 'their' tank would also feature the names of three of the savings groups which had contributed.

In September, Wing Commander Kayll, DSO, DFC, managed to escape from his PoW camp with a companion, and the two walked for seven days before being captured. Kayll was subsequently moved to Oflag XI at Schubin in Poland. Refusing to be discouraged he helped to organise further escape attempts.

The firm of W. Doxford & Sons Ltd. had weathered the recession largely due to its reputation and through the popularity of its innovative Doxford Economy tramp, first launched in 1934, and its Improved Doxford Economy tramp, first launched in 1938. By 1942, the company had been steadily investing in both facilities and workforce and had constructed new sheds, stores, lofts and a new canteen for workers. The company was busy throughout the war and made a massive contribution to the national war effort with its busiest period coming in 1942 when new records were set for production.

One of the shipyards which had fallen victim to the slump of the 1930s was that of Swan, Hunter & Wigham Richardson Ltd. at Southwick. A name far more associated with the River Tyne, the firm had opened a four-berth yard at Southwick in 1912 in order to take the pressure off their Tyne yards and to

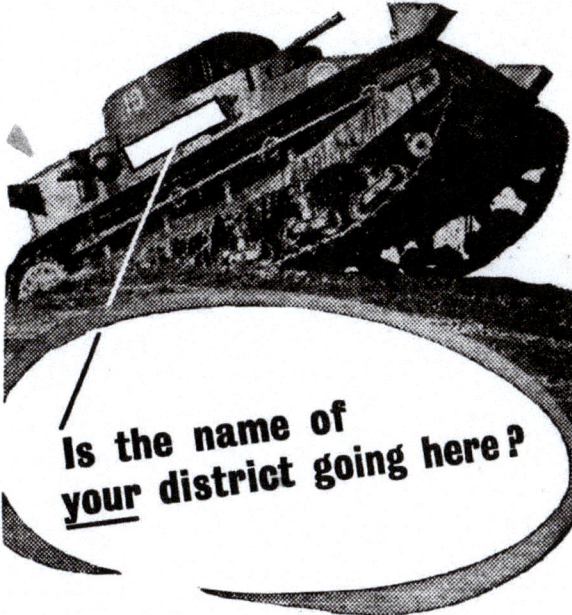

Tanks for Attack campaign poster (Sunderland Echo)

build the excess orders of colliers and coasters (largely for British companies), and steamers for the Great Lakes. The Southwick yard also constructed floating docks and had built several merchantmen during the First World War. The yard, however, had been mothballed for two years in 1921 but more orders allowed the yard to be reopened and to remain open until the slump of the early 1930s, when orders dried up. The final ship to be built at the yard was the collier *Flathouse*, completed in 1931. The yard, like many others, was purchased by National Shipbuilders Security Ltd. and partly dismantled. By mid-1942, however, the losses of merchant shipping, especially in the Battle of the Atlantic, were reaching catastrophic levels and it was decided that some few yards that had been closed might be reopened and semi and unskilled workers put to work on constructing vessels which were largely prefabricated and required less skill. Joseph L. Thompson & Sons Ltd. sent a large team of workers to the now derelict yard and three berths were rebuilt to go alongside the administration block and the joiners' shop which still remained. The company also transferred a large amount of equipment from its North Sands yard.

By mid-1942, the shipbuilding industry was coming under increasing criticism and scrutiny over allegations of slackness, corruption and poor working practices. The Select Committee on National Expenditure therefore launched an enquiry into the industry and reported back later in the year. The report of the committee did highlight problems within the industry but the majority of Wear shipyard companies believed that the industry had, in fact, passed with a relatively clean bill of health.

One of the main criticisms contained within the report was that the reopening of old, disused, yards should have been a priority and had been performed too slowly and inconsistently. This, argued the shipyard companies, not unconvincingly, was a fault of government policy and nothing to do with them. Indeed, the Wearside shipbuilders could point to the fact that this had been urged all along by themselves and by other shipbuilding companies in the north-east. Indeed, there had been delegations sent to London to argue for the reopening of derelict yards.

Another criticism was that there had been too great a concentration on the production of marine engines rather than in expanding shipbuilding capacity. The shipyard-owners agreed that labour difficulties could probably have been averted if greater dilution had been undertaken more speedily alongside an earlier introduction of female labour, but pointed out that in the first years of the war, construction of marine engines had lagged far behind construction of hulls and had created a bottleneck which they had only recently solved. They did agree, however, that expansion should have taken place hand-in-hand with solving the engine bottleneck problem.

Against allegations of slacking amongst some men who knew that they were in a reserved occupation and felt that they now had more bargaining power than ever before, the shipbuilders claimed that, while it might be worthwhile to appoint a yard committee to decide on allegations of slacking and with the power to recommend de-reservation of particular individuals, although it would be popular that slackers be de-reserved and called up there was a possibility that some young, skilled, workers who were eager to serve in uniform, especially in the RAF, 'which has a great attraction for them', would realise that by slacking they would be de-reserved and eligible for military service. This would denude shipyards of valuable workers and adversely affect output.

One of the most frequent allegations made against shipyard workers was that they were persistently guilty of 'knocking off' early, i.e. stopping work before the designated time. The Wear shipbuilders, while admitting that this was a problem, said that in their area it was most often the piece-workers who practised this and that it was often with good cause. They explained that the piece-workers, paid by results, often saw this as being their own business, especially if they had a good reason. Many times such a worker would realise that it was infeasible to begin a new piece of work with only 10-15 minutes of a shift remaining and that therefore it was also pointless to be hanging around the yard doing nothing until the end of the shift. Far better, argued the shipbuilders, that he make his way home where he would be able to rest or possibly even prepare himself to take part in Home Guard duties or in digging in garden or allotment. The employers were at pains to point out, however, that this did not apply to hourly paid workers such as electricians, painters and plumbers who should remain until the official end of shift at all times. Other reasons for workers leaving work before the end of the shift included the fact that many piece-workers were involved in very heavy labour meaning that they could not wear watches and with the wartime ban on work hooters and buzzers very often did not know the exact time. This was combined with the fact that many more workers were now dependent on public transport to reach home and were naturally anxious to be at the gates in time to catch their bus with failure to do so resulting in a lengthy walk home and perhaps no meal at the end of it.

The Select Committee had also been critical of the resistance to the employment of women in the shipyards and the Wear shipbuilders were forced to admit that only 300 or so women were employed in the industry in the area. They argued that this was due to the nature of shipbuilding work, meaning that the majority of those who were working were employed in general labouring and painting, with a few rivet heating. They argued that there were not many jobs in the industry in which a woman might be gainfully employed.

The unions generally backed the claims of the employers with one representative of the Boilermakers' Society telling the committee that there were no problems on the Wear, that everybody was 'working wonderfully well, and the output is greater than ever it has been'. The official went on to cite the attitude towards overtime amongst the workforce, arguing that if weekend overtime work was necessary, the situation need only be explained to the workers and they would readily agree to work. Indeed, he claimed that one young man had complained to him that he was not being allowed to work enough overtime. He worked in a boiler shop where overtime had been limited to two half shifts per week and he felt that this rule should be overturned, so keen was he to contribute to the war effort.

Even the committee was forced to admit that while there was some cause for complaint, this was slight and that an excellent job was being performed in both merchant shipbuilding and in repair work, with output per worker never having been so high. It was also admitted that in shipbuilding circles the Wear was, in some ways, seen as leading the way. The levels of cooperation achieved between employers and employees on Wearside came in for particular praise with one trade union delegate who had recently attended a large conference in the capital returning home to Sunderland 'convinced that the Wear was three years ahead of other districts'.[33]

One Sunderland woman was bucking the trend of only semi- or non-skilled female labour being employed in the Wearside shipyards. Mrs Florence Collard had suffered severely during the war so far. Her husband was away in the forces and she had been bombed out in Plymouth before moving back to Sunderland. She was then bombed out in a raid on Sunderland and for some time was trapped in the wreckage of her house before being rescued and going back to her shift at Bartram & Sons Ltd. Mrs Collard had found employment at the shipyard as a welder and became the first woman in the area to join the Boilermakers' Society (albeit on a temporary membership). Even in the example of the plucky Mrs Collard, however, an attitude towards women workers was

Mrs Florence Collard, welder at Bartram & Sons Ltd and the first woman to locally join the Boilermakers' Society (Sunderland Echo)

revealed when an official at the shipyard assured people that Mrs Collard was not employed on working on hulls or tanks and was found welding work at ground level.

December brought news of the death of another Sunderland man who was serving in the RN. Engine Room Artificer 3rd Class James Kent Ragg was serving aboard the *Abdiel*-Class minelayer HMS *Manxman* in the Mediterranean. On 1 December, the minelayer was travelling between Algiers and Gibraltar when she was torpedoed by U-375. Severely damaged and with several of her crew, including Ragg, killed, the stricken vessel managed to limp back to port at Oran. Engine Room Artificer 3rd Class Ragg was buried at sea and is commemorated on the Chatham Naval Memorial.[34] On 29 December, the unfortunate sailor was remembered in the roll of honour of the *Sunderland Echo* with a short commemorative piece placed in the newspaper by his aunt Ethel, uncle Fred and his cousins, Yvonne (who was in the WAAF) and Kenneth.

CHAPTER 5

1943: The Last Blitz

❖

We have already heard of the successful mission undertaken by Mr Cyril Thompson of Joseph L. Thompson & Sons Ltd. and Harry Hunter of the North Eastern Marine Engineering Co. Ltd. in 1940, and in the first weeks of 1943 the two men journeyed north into Canada where an initial order for twenty 'Empire' type vessels, known in Canada as the 'Fort' type, were secured. This eventually led to 300 of the type being built in Canada.

For many Sunderland families the wartime conditions of living in Britain were exacerbated by anxiety over the fate of loved ones serving in the forces in far-flung theatres of operation, where news home was infrequent and unpredictable. Many Sunderland men were serving in the desert and had participated in the success at El-Alamein in late November 1942. One, Sergeant Albert Dunn of the 6th Battalion, DLI, had won the MM at the battle. He was notified of his award as he lay in hospital, recovering from a poisoned arm.

Following the Battle of the Mareth Line in March, the family and friends of Sergeant Dunn, MM, would no doubt have been pleased to find that his photograph was featured in the *Daily Mirror* alongside a caption which stated that he had been one of the first NCOs to reach the Mareth Line positions. Sergeant Dunn (24) was the third son of Mr and Mrs F. Dunn of Laura Street, Sunderland. Before the war, he had been employed at Jobling's Pyrex Works and was known around the town as a keen sportsman, with a strong interest in football, cricket and cycling. He had enlisted in the army in October 1939.

Sergeant Albert Dunn, MM, 6th DLI (Daily Mirror)

Yet another Sunderland airman lost his life when Bristol Beaufighter *X8064* of 235 Squadron crashed into the North Sea off Leuchars on 3 May. The squadron had sent a force to attack German shipping off the Norwegian coast but, when 7 miles off Leuchar, the Beaufighter was seen to spin after attempting a turn. The pilot was seen to make three attempts to recover from the spin but the aircraft hit the sea, killing the two crewmen. The pilot was Sergeant Wyndham Greenwood of 4 Newbold Avenue, Sunderland.

The troublesome PoW, Wing Commander Kayll, was once again moved, this time to Stalag Luft 3. Shortly after his arrival here he was placed in charge of the escape committee for the east compound. Escape activities were ever-present in this camp and this increased the dangers for those who organised such attempts. Kayll refused to be cowed and organised the security and intelligence section of the camp escape committee. One of the greatest successes during Kayll's time in camp was the wooden horse escape which saw several escapers use a gymnastic horse as cover for their tunnelling.

Sunderland had experienced steady small-scale raids throughout March, but April had passed relatively quietly, as had the beginning of May. On the night of Saturday, 15 May, the population retired to bed, no doubt hoping that the recent series of small raids had come to an end; they were wrong. At approximately 1.45am, they were awoken by the now very familiar wail of the sirens and wearily took to their shelters once more. This, however, was to be no nuisance raid but a heavy and concentrated raid which focused on the city and surrounding area. By the time the all-clear sounded at 3.09am, very severe damage had been caused and Sunderland and the immediate surrounding area had suffered at least 110 civilians killed along with massive property damage. At least 75 of the fatalities were endured in the town itself, while 73 people were seriously injured and 125 injured less severely. In Sunderland itself, 200 houses were destroyed with a further 10,000 damaged.

Property Damage in Sunderland Following Raid of 16 May.

Property Type	Details	Destroyed	Damaged
Food Stores	Retailers	7	67
	Licensed Premises	3	11
	Breweries	1	
	Cafes	1	
	Factories	1	
	Dairies	1	
	Wholesalers	2	
Churches		6	
Houses		200	10,000
Theatres		1	
Misc. Industrial Concerns		12	

The raid lasted for less than two hours but was a heavy one with the ARP HQ at Thornholme later listing at least 124 separate incidents of bombs impacting within the boundaries of the town. Amongst these were several 1,000kg high-explosive bombs and a number of the widely feared parachute mines.

As was usual in these raids, the human cost was particularly moving when entire families were involved. At 1 Parkside Terrace, Roker, a 500kg bomb had caused extensive damage, including destroying the water main which disrupted the gas supply, and resulted in the deaths of George Henry Haswell (36), a member of the National Fire Service (NFS), his wife, Gladys Hunt Haswell (35) and their two sons, David Dixon Haswell (6) and 12-day-old Norman. The youngster was to have been christened the next day at the church which lay just doors away. At no. 4, Isabella Coxon (85) was killed. At Atkinson Road in Fulwell a 1,000kg bomb resulted in the deaths of six members of the Miller family at no. 90. They were James Miller (47) and his wife Gladys May (45), along with their four sons: Gordon (16); Denis (12); Alan Geoffrey (9); and Eric (5). The Thompson family of 2 Barracks Cottages lost four members on that terrible night. They were George Irwing Thompson (30), his wife Mary Doreen (27) and their two children, George (5) and Doris (3).

Those whose duties led to them being exposed to the full dangers of an air raid continued to pay a price for their courage. Two Sunderland fire guards were killed: Lucy Suffield (51) lost her life at 10 Azalea Avenue; and Robert L. Goldsmith (54) was killed at Atkinson Road, Fulwell. Special Constable Lancelot C. Slawther was killed at Roker Baths Road, and first aid party member William H. Kennard was killed at 79 Cooper Street, Roker, when a 250kg bomb exploded at the junction of Cooper Street and Givens Street.

An elderly man, Leslie Jeffries Salter (80), and his wife, Elsie Gertrude Salter (55), were both killed at 12 Azalea Avenue. The Salters' bodies were buried in the ruins of their house for some time before being recovered. Other fatalities included Mr Joseph Taylor (53), who lost his life at 25 Alexandra Park.

At the yard of Joseph L. Thompson & Sons Ltd. the tramp SS *Denewood* was being fitted out at Manor Quay and was damaged by either shrapnel or machine-gun fire.

Amongst the stories which emerged in the immediate aftermath of the raid was the story of Jimmy Laidler (17) who had unwittingly become a human prop in a bomb-wrecked terrace house. When rescue squads arrived and began their recovery attempt they reached the unconscious Jimmy first but realised that his body was shoring up a large boulder and that, if they moved him, the whole property could collapse, killing those who remained trapped beyond. For several hours, the rescue workers extricated survivors before they were finally able to remove Jimmy and rush him to hospital. This was at Waterloo Place, Monkwearmouth, where eleven people were killed at nos. 2-5. There is some confusion over the identity of the human prop as the account given above is from the *Daily Mirror* of 17 May while other accounts name him as Robson.

Fatalities at Waterloo Place, Monkwearmouth, on 16 May.

Name	Age	House No.
Albert Alcock	53	5
Emily Jane Alcock	50	5
Mary Jane Alcock	84	5
John Feeney	9	4
Mary Elizabeth Feeney	12	4
Edward Innins	52	5
Elizabeth Ann Laidler	52	4
Patricia Robson	2	3
Evelyn Thwaites	17	2
Mary Thwaites	10	2
Sarah Jane Thwaites	43	2

Mr John Feeney was an air raid warden who was found suffering from very serious injuries at the edge of the crater which had been blown into the road at Waterloo Place, two of his children were killed. A fellow warden, Mr Robert Thwaites was also injured, he lost two sisters and his mother at no.2.

Badly affected areas nearby included Seaham Harbour where a parachute mine exploded resulting in thirty-four deaths and seriously injuring forty-two. Twelve houses were demolished and a further ten seriously damaged and several people were trapped for some time. Two hundred people had to be accommodated in rest centres and the electricity supply was disrupted due to damage to overhead cables. No fewer than eighteen people lost their lives on Viceroy Street. Amongst the dead were four members of the Home Guard. Three were killed on the same street, John Thomas Davison (35) and Wrightson Kirk Cuthbert (28) were both killed at 28 Viceroy Street; while John Bell (35) was killed at no. 48. Also killed at no. 28 were five members of the Corkhill family: Gerald (32); Barbara Dixon Corkhill (28); Alan (6); Marion (4); and 11-month-old June. Rescue workers battled for thirteen hours, tunnelling through 12ft of debris and a 14in brick wall, to rescue Mary Kelly (19) and George Corkhill (7). Miss Kelly was badly injured and first-aid workers battled to help her while efforts at rescue continued. Other fatalities at Seaham included Air Raid Warden George William Weir (43) who was killed at Sophia Street and Mrs Violet Daisy Shaw (54), who died of shock at the same location.

The village of Offerton was shaken by the explosion of a parachute mine and it was determined that another had fallen close by but failed to explode. Several houses in the village were damaged, while the unexploded mine resulted in the closure of the Penshaw to Sunderland railway line and two minor roads. The unexploded mine lay so close to the village that the entire population was evacuated.

With so much property damage and with unexploded bombs causing the evacuation of hundreds more civilians, it was necessary for nine rest centres to be opened in order to cope with the accommodation and feeding of 660 people. Due to the breakdown in communications, which developed as the raid continued, the Ministry of Information loudspeaker vans were used to disseminate information alongside the facilities of

Rediffusion Ltd., who allowed the controller to broadcast using their relay system.

In the immediate aftermath of the raid, administration centres were opened at St Mary's RC School, Bishopwearmouth church hall and Monkwearmouth Central School. The staff in these centres were available to give advice and information on a variety of subjects relating to the air raid and by the end of the day they had dealt with 6,000 enquiries. The authorities quickly managed to find billets for 1,298 people (550 families) from the north side of the river and 678 from the south side (230 families) who had been rendered homeless by the raid.

Work gangs over 1,000 strong were working throughout Sunday and Monday (16/17 May) to try to repair the extensive damage inflicted on property and critical infrastructure. Considerable damage had been done to the town's water supply system and, although many areas had their supplies restored in the hours following the raid, the residents of Roker were without water for several days and had to be supplied by water carts. The town's sewage system was also damaged. Electricity supplies throughout the town were also badly disrupted. Once again, the majority of damage was repaired quite quickly but at Fulwell the NESCo network had been more severely damaged and this meant that the area was without any electricity for almost eleven hours. The Marley Potts and High Southwick areas lost their supply of electricity for even longer. Surprisingly, the gas supply got off fairly lightly although supplies were disrupted for 200 houses in the Roker area as a result of a burst water main but the situation was rectified by 18 May.

Propaganda leaflets were also dropped during the course of the raid. These were concerned with what they described as the true scale of losses to allied merchant shipping, clearly aimed specifically at an area with a keen interest in the topic. They were, however, not entirely effective given that several of the 412 ships which it listed as having been sunk since 1941 were actually in port nearby (either on the Tyne or Wear) at the time of the raid.

Defences were not exactly at their best during the raid and the enemy force lost only one aircraft. A Dornier 217 K-1 of

6/KG2 was shot down 35 miles off the Sunderland coast by a Bristol Beaufighter night-fighter of 604 Squadron at 2.15am. The bodies of two of the crew were recovered from the sea while two remained missing.[35] The Luftwaffe reported three bombers had failed to return but these losses may have been conflated with a raid which had been conducted on East Anglia earlier in the evening and which had resulted in the loss of two aircraft.

The reporting of the raid was somewhat muted with wartime censorship meaning that it was not admitted that the town had been the target of attack for some time, despite clear German claims. All that was acknowledged in the immediate aftermath was that a town in the north of England had been raided and that there had been a heavy death toll.

Accounts in the local press on 17 May focused mainly on the lies which had been found in the four-page propaganda leaflets which had been dropped during the raid. Buried within the account was the acknowledgement that the 'final casualty list may be a fairly heavy one' and that 'There was some damage to industrial premises, but house property suffered severely, and several churches were damaged and a theatre destroyed.' The account did go on to describe how, despite a furious anti-aircraft barrage, the raiders swooped in to drop flares and then bombs 'which started fires in several areas. Works were destroyed and a cinema blazed for some hours.' The unfortunate fate of six of the Miller family was mentioned, along with the fact that another son, James, was currently serving in Rhodesia with the RAF.

German radio stated that Sunderland had been raided for the thirty-seventh time and that it was an important military target as the docks and shipyards there carried out repairs on damaged vessels while also building tankers and merchant vessels. The account described how the bombers had been able to accurately locate and identify their targets because of clear skies and good visibility. The broadcast also described how bombing had taken place from a low altitude and that 'hits were scored on docks and wharves … explosions were followed by several large fires which spread rapidly'.[36] The account concluded with an account by a German pilot who, it was claimed, had flown on the raid. He claimed that although it was a difficult operation it was carried out successfully. The Germans' propaganda claims regarding daring bomber raids, however, were quickly eclipsed.

Elsewhere, Home Guards were parading to celebrate the third birthday of the creation of the force. Those in Sunderland, however, were involved with clearing up the debris of the raid and in rescuing those who were still believed to be trapped in the wreckage of houses. The clear-up was accompanied by the oddly unfamiliar sound of pealing church bells which were rung to celebrate the recent victory in Tunisia.

There was one final fatality of the raid. Mrs Mary Nelson (36) was living in Newcastle but was in Sunderland on the night of the raid visiting family. She was last reported as having been seen running from her family's home across the street to warn an old lady, who was deaf, of the danger. Mary was posted missing, but her battered body was later recovered from the debris and she was taken to hospital. Mrs Nelson died of her injuries on 10 June.

Although the relatively amateurish propaganda attempts made during the raid had been ridiculed for inaccuracy, the fact was that losses to merchant shipping continued to be heavy and Sunderland men continued to pay the price. On the day following the raid, yet another Sunderland member of the merchant navy lost his life. Dennis Johnson (22) was a junior engineering officer aboard the cargo motor vessel MV *Northmoor*. The vessel had been built by William Doxford & Sons at Sunderland in 1928 and was owned by the Newcastle-based Moor Line owned by Sir Walter Runciman & Co. Ltd. On 17 May, she was part of the six-ship Convoy LMD-17 bound for Buenos Aires via Durban with a load of 6,912 tons of coal. At 2.12pm, while north of Durban, she was torpedoed and sunk by U-198. Twelve of her thirty-nine-man crew lost their lives in the incident, including Mr Johnson.[37]

The next day brought the death of another Sunderland merchant mariner. Second Engineering Officer Stephen Rose (59) was serving aboard the SS *Empire Eve* when she was sunk off the coast of Algeria. The SS *Empire Eve* was a catapult aircraft merchant (CAM) ship built as a stop-gap to escort convoys while at the same time carrying cargo. She had been built in 1941 by the Sunderland firm of William Pickersgill & Sons Ltd. On 18 May, the ship was carrying 6,500 tons of coal and 150 tons of lubricating oil as part of Convoy KMS 14 bound for Algeria from Gibraltar. She was sunk by U-414 off the coast of Algeria with the loss of five of her eighty-seven-man crew. Second Engineering Officer Rose was a married man and is commemorated on the Tower Hill Memorial.

In the days after the raid on Sunderland, news broke of the hugely inspirational Dambusters raid which had been carried out on the night of 16/17 May. Many of the residents of Sunderland were still reeling from the after-effects of the recent raid but many were buoyed by the news of this daring strike which had caused such devastation in Germany's industrial heartland.

MV Northmoor, *sunk off Durban with the loss of twelve lives. (City of Vancouver Archives)*

SS Empire Eve, *clearly showing the launch ramp on her bow. (Unknown)*

Others received bad news which they must have anticipated for some time but which when it came, shattered remaining faint hopes for the survival of a loved one. In the days following the 16 May raid, the Skipsey family from the tiny village of Haswell Plough learned that their son, Sergeant John Skipsey had been confirmed as having lost his life on 18 August 1942. It was later revealed that the Wellington bomber in which Sergeant Skipsey was the rear gunner had crashed near Kimswerd, Holland, and that the six-man crew had all been killed and subsequently buried at Wonseradeel (Kimswerd) Protestant Churchyard. It is suspected that the Wellington was shot down by a night-fighter piloted by Oberleutnant Ludwig Becker of 6/NJG2.

Sergeant John Skipsey, killed on a raid to Osnabruck (Sunderland Echo)

While the tide of the war appeared to be turning in the Allies favour, the people of Sunderland were still on alert after the recent severe air raid and their fears were realised in the early hours of 24 May, when another heavy attack developed over much of the north-east. Once again this was a short but sharp raid which lasted about an hour but during the course of it 11 parachute mines, 67 high-explosive bombs, 9 firepot high-explosive bombs, 3 phosphorous incendiary bombs and approximately 600 incendiary bombs fell onto the town.

This proved to be the deadliest raid on the town during the course of the war with eighty-four people losing their lives and twenty-two being injured. Once again, damage to property was severe with 310 houses being destroyed, 1,000 seriously damaged and 10,000 being damaged less severely. In addition to this, eight churches and chapels were damaged along with three theatres and picture houses and a number of schools were damaged with nine having to be closed. Thirteen rest centres were opened in the aftermath of the raid and they accommodated 3,000 people. Twelve emergency feeding centres were also opened and these provided meals for 3,791 people of the town. Once again, the administrative centres were opened to enable people to find out information and to try to trace loved ones. Food stores and suppliers were also badly hit, with a total of 208 being either destroyed or damaged.

Food Centres Damaged or Destroyed in the Raid of 24 May.

Category	Destroyed	Badly Damaged	Slightly Damaged
Retailers & Caterers	12	14	137
Wholesalers	2	1	3
Factories & Depots	2	1	2
Licensed Premises	1	7	26
TOTALS	17	23	168

This second serious raid resulted in more serious damage to several important shipyards and works within the town and in the nearby area. A ship was also sunk in the river after being hit by bombs, and two which were berthed in South Dock were damaged.

Damage to the infrastructure of the town was again severe, with water mains once more being fractured and the supply stopped for some time in the Hendon area. Yet again arrangements had to be made for supplies to be brought in by cart. In other areas, temporary by-pass pipes were set up to restore supplies until damage to mains caused by bomb craters could be made good and more complete repairs carried out. The gas supply in the town was also affected, with damage to several mains resulting in many areas facing low pressure supplies for approximately a day. The sewers were also damaged and repair gangs put to work in the immediate aftermath of the raid. These gangs were assisted in their work by reinforcements which were sought and supplied by several neighbouring authorities including Gateshead, Newcastle and South Shields. During the raid itself and in the aftermath, ARP services were supplemented by colleagues from the Northumberland and County Durham areas. To feed these extra workers, the town's mobile canteens were pressed into service and reinforcements obtained from other communities in County Durham.

Once more the ARP services, police and Home Guard paid a heavy price for their courage in going about their duties during the raid. No fewer than seven fire guards or firewatchers were killed during the raid. They were joined by three members of the Home Guard, two members of the St John Ambulance Brigade, an air raid warden and a member of the Police War Reserve.

ARP Workers, Home Guard and others killed on duty during the Raid.

Name	Age	Location	Duty
John W. Annison	41	Ravensworth Street	St John Ambulance
Thomas Edward Ewes	41	Alexandra Bridge	Police War Reserve
George Forster	50	Lodge Terrace Shelter	Home Guard
Maurice Gallerstein	19	8 Salem Avenue	Home Guard
Ernest Godsworthy	46	15 St Abbs Street	Fire Guard
George Robert Johnson	61	Dalton-le-Dale	ARP Post ARP Warden
David Patrick Lorenson	66	Lodge Terrace	Fire Guard
John Sillett	45	14 St Abbs Street	Fire Guard
John Cutter Simpson	23	4 Devonshire Street	Fire Guard
Percy Stoker	60	17 West Terrace, Ryhope	Firewatcher
Thomas Thompson	50	71 Alexandra Road	Fire Guard
Winifred Tuddenham	47	6 Salem Avenue	St John Ambulance
Robert Bewick Ward	56	Ashmore Terrace	Home Guard
George Henry J. Whittle	40	Running Street	Fire Guard

Shortly after 3.00am, several firepot-type incendiaries fell onto Murton Colliery's stone heap but caused no damage. Half the bombs failed to detonate and were later removed for investigation. At the same time six high-explosive bombs fell on Cold Heseldon, with one scoring a direct hit on a small transformer house at an electricity substation. Of the other bombs, four exploded but caused only minor damage while one failed to explode. A parachute mine fell on the small village of Dalton-le-Dale but although it failed to explode, air raid warden George Robert Johnson (61) died at his post in the village, reportedly of shock. Shortly afterwards, Ryhope Colliery suffered severe damage when two 500kg bombs fell on it. Damage was mainly to buildings and plant and was so bad that the colliery had to close down for some time while repairs were made. At the same time, nine firepot bombs fell in the colliery yard resulting in minor fire damage. A firewatcher, Mr Percy Stoker (40) was killed at 17 West Terrace, Ryhope, during the incident.

Once again, the vagaries of fate played a large role in determining who lost their lives and who survived. Particularly unfortunate were a group of joiners from Glasgow who had been brought down to the area to make repairs following the earlier raid, some were killed when a bomb hit their lodgings.

Serious damage was also caused to several of the shipyards, with facilities such as canteens and offices being destroyed or badly damaged. Amongst the hardest hit was the yard of Joseph L. Thompson & Sons Ltd., which suffered severe damage when bombs wrecked the offices and boardroom as well as causing heavy damage to the shops and plant elsewhere in the yard. The SS *Denewood*, damaged in the earlier air raid, suffered a direct hit from a parachute mine and was sunk at her moorings, while the *Chinese Prince*, which was lying alongside and also being fitted out, was damaged.

We may remember the 1940 marriage of Sunderland-born Sergeant John Norman Donald, RAF. After his marriage, the trainee pilot was posted to Canada for pilot training and earned his wings as a flight sergeant at the beginning of 1942 but was retained as an instructor before being posted back to Britain where, in July, he was commissioned as a pilot officer. Donald had obviously been very successful in his training and had since proven himself as an able and skilled pilot. Perhaps his pre-war upbringing, being educated at Sunderland Junior Technical School and Technical College, had helped him in his new career. By the summer of 1943, he had been appointed to a prestigious position as a service test pilot for the firm of Gloster Aircraft Ltd.

Another family to receive the terrible news of the death of a loved one was the Paterson family of Pallion. Mrs Gladys Paterson (née Elder) had known that her husband had been reported missing in Java in March 1942 but since then neither she nor her husband's parents, George and Alice, had received any further news of the fate of Gunner Robert Paterson, 242 Battery, 48th Light Anti-Aircraft (LAA) Regiment, Royal Artillery. It was revealed in early August that Gunner Paterson (34) had died on 18 May 1943, while in Japanese captivity. The 48th LAA Regiment had sailed from Gourock in 1941 (on the day that Japan declared war) and had arrived at Java in early 1942 just in time for the Japanese invasion. The regiment was overrun, despite a heroic defence, and suffered heavy casualties on 1 March 1942, but it seems that Gunner Paterson escaped this onslaught and his surrender was later reported to have occurred on 8 March. Before the war, he had been employed as a labourer and his wife must have feared the worst when the telegram arrived at her home at 12 St Luke's Road, Pallion. The account of Gunner Paterson's death was that he died of beriberi and while this may well be true it is known that he was imprisoned in a Japanese work camp on Borneo. The conditions in these camps, under the command of Lieutenant Colonel Suga, were appalling and thousands perished or were executed by their captors. Gunner Paterson is buried at Labuan War Cemetery alongside 3,922 other poor souls.[38]

Following the successful conclusion of the North African campaign in mid-May, many of the Sunderland men who had fought their way through the desert campaigns found themselves now tasked with the invasion of Sicily. The campaign to capture the island involved 160,000 Allied servicemen and was seen as a prelude to the impending invasion of mainland Italy. We have already encountered Sunderland-born NCO Sergeant Albert Dunn, MM. By August 1943, Sergeant Dunn found himself involved in the fighting in Sicily. While the Italians had offered little opposition, the Germans put up a fierce resistance. The fighting to take the town of Catania and the battle for the Simeto River bridgehead was particularly fierce and there were heavy casualties. Sergeant Dunn was killed on 11 August and was buried at the Catania War Cemetery.

With its long tradition of glassmaking, many of Sunderland's products were used in various capacities in the war effort. The Wear Glass Works of James A. Jobling & Co. Ltd. became world-famous for its Pyrex glass. The firm manufactured armoured glass, which was extensively used in the aircraft industry. It was not only the RAF that made use of this product, the United States Army Air Force (USAAF), and particularly the 8th USAAF, which was based in Britain, made extensive use of the material in fitting replacement glass to its aircraft. In August, a number of workers from the factory were invited to a USAAF base to inspect the aircraft and be shown how their products were put

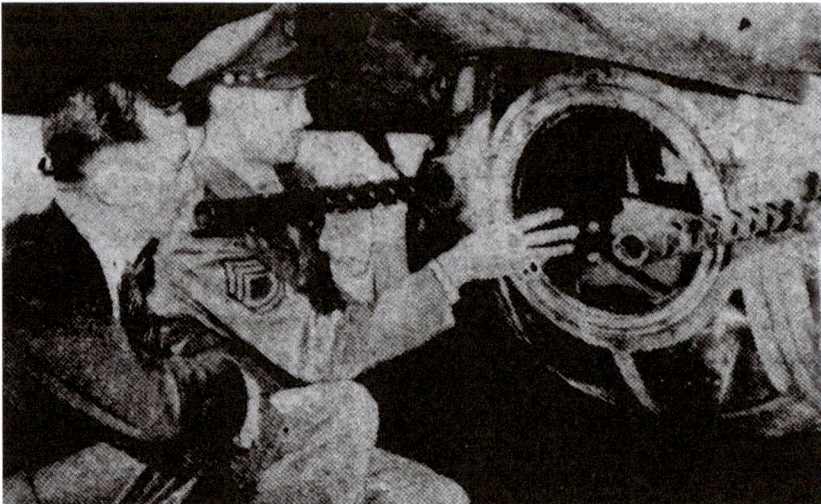

USAAF First Sergeant shows bullet-proof glass in ball turret of B-17 to Mr Robson of the Wear Glass Works (Sunderland Echo)

to use in taking the war to Germany. Amongst the visitors was former Ferryhill miner, Mr John James Robson. Included in his tour was an in-depth inspection of a B-17 Flying Fortress where he was shown how the bulletproof glass he helped produce was fitted in the ball turret of a B-17 with the details being explained by the first sergeant who manned the turret.

On 21 October, Pilot Officer Norman Gilbert Donald, RAF, took off from the Gloster Aircraft Ltd. airfield at Brockworth in Gloucestershire to test a newly produced Albemarle II (*V1741*). Accompanying Pilot Officer Donald were a Mr T. Timms and two young air cadets, J.F.S. Cheriton and L.W. White, who were along for an air experience flight. As the Albemarle approached the Gloster facility at 3,000ft to land, it entered a left turn and was seen to begin an increasingly steep dive. The dive was recovered but the aircraft struck the ground flat and at a very high speed and exploded into flames after hitting an orchard; all aboard were killed. There is some slight confusion over the role in which Pilot Officer Donald was now flying, as the Commonwealth

An Armstrong Whitworth Albermarle I, similar to that in which Pilot Officer Donald lost his life (Public Domain)

War Graves Commission lists him as being a test pilot for Gloster Aircraft Ltd. while other sources list him as being a test pilot for Armstrong Whitworth at the time of his death.[39] On Tuesday, 26 October, the young widow of Pilot Officer Donald accompanied his funeral cortege from Sunderland to Newcastle where his remains were cremated amidst a service replete with full military honours. Like many a wartime wedding, their story had ended in tragedy.

On a more cheerful note, it was announced in October that a Sunderland-born sailor was to be awarded a Bar to an earlier DSM. Chief Stoker A. Lawrence had survived the sinking of HMS *Royal Oak* in 1939 and had subsequently served on a trawler, but for the past three years had served aboard a destroyer. His DSM had been awarded in 1942 for his part in the action in the Channel when the German battleship *Scharnhorst* managed to escape the Royal Navy. In November 1942, he had been wounded in another engagement in the Channel. Stoker Lawrence's widowed mother still lived in Pallion, at 7 Tanfield Street, while his wife and children lived at the family home in Southsea. Upon being invited to what would be his second investiture ceremony at Buckingham Palace, the family decided that since his wife had attended the first, the honour of accompanying him to this second ceremony should fall to his two eldest children.

Not all of the casualties suffered by Sunderland were due to enemy action. We have already seen how men could be killed during training or in accidents, but on 7 November a Sunderland man lost his life at the hands of a comrade. Leading Seaman Richard Stokell (24) was a seven-year naval veteran and was serving aboard the anti-aircraft ship HMS *Ulster Queen*. Born at Monkwearmouth, Leading Seaman Stokell had worked at the Wear Glass Works before joining the Royal Navy. He had been married

Chief Stoker A. Lawrence, DSM and Bar (Sunderland Echo)

in 1940 and left behind his widow, Dorothy, and a young child, as well as his parents, George and Margaret. On the night he lost his life, the *Ulster Queen* was berthed at Gibraltar. It would seem that Leading Seaman Stokell and a Rating, Henry Adolphus Loram (23), had got into an argument in the mess and that this had ended up in a violent confrontation during which Loram stabbed Stokell in the abdomen. Loram was taken into custody and charged with murder but a verdict of manslaughter was returned by the jury and Loram, of Higher Brixham, Devon, was sentenced to eighteen months' imprisonment with hard labour. Leading Seaman Stokell's widow later received a letter from her husband's crewmates expressing, on behalf of the officers and crew of the ship, the deep sorrow and sympathy over his loss. The letter also informed Mrs Stokell that her husband had been buried at sea with full military honours.[40]

We have already seen how the derelict shipyard formerly owned by Swan, Hunter & Wigham Richardson had been reopened by Joseph L. Thompson & Sons Ltd. The first vessel launched from the yard, now renamed the National Shipbuilding Corporation (Wear) yard, was the 7,038 ton SS *Empire Trail*, a 'D' type ship, which was launched in August and completed in December.[41] The yard went on to make a modest contribution of a total of five tramp vessels during the course of the war.

The Deptford yard of Sir James Laing & Sons Ltd remained extremely busy throughout the year. The tanker specialist was very heavily engaged in building ships for government orders but during the course of the year two tankers for private owners were also launched. These were the 'Norwegian' type *Wearfield* and the *Thamesfield*.

The yard of Bartram & Sons Ltd. experienced its busiest wartime year in 1943. During the year, the company completed five tramp freighters and also carried out extensive conversion work on four ships in order to equip them for Russian convoy work. Repair work was also undertaken and the company embarked on a process of building at its site, which resulted in the construction of a new berth, platers' shed, welding shed and the purchasing of new 15-ton electric travelling jib cranes.

CHAPTER 6

1944: The End in Sight?

❖

As the Bomber Command campaign against Berlin continued, the loss of life amongst the aircrew of the Command continued to rise. No doubt the men of the Command were exhausted when they were ordered to attack the German capital once more on the night of 1 January as, for many, this would be the second Berlin raid in four nights and the third in just over a week and they were probably hoping for a quiet New Year's night. The attack on this night saw 421 Lancasters take off for the target. (The Halifax bomber force had been temporarily rested as they had suffered such heavy casualties on recent raids.) The raid proved to be a disappointment, as heavy cloud once again obscured the city and the scattered nature of the bombing resulted in only twenty-one houses and one industrial building being destroyed according to German reports. The Luftwaffe night-fighters infiltrated the bomber stream long before the target was reached and several planes were seen to be shot down although only two were lost over the target itself. The experienced crew of Flight Lieutenant D.A. MacDonald, DFC, RCAF, of 630 Squadron, had taken off from RAF East Kirby but failed to return. Subsequent enquiries revealed that their Lancaster III (*JB532, LE-X*) had been homebound after bombing the target when it was hit by flak which blew one engine completely out of the airframe. The bomber dived steeply and crashed at Grossbeuthen, killing all eight men aboard. The bomb aimer was Flight Sergeant John Mowbray Turnbull (22). The young airman was a native of Sunderland and left behind his parents, George and Edith.[42]

Flight Sergeant Turnbull was one of at least two Sunderland airmen to be killed on that night's raid. The other was Sergeant Thomas Henry Mallett (20). Sergeant Mallett was the mid-upper gunner in Lancaster III (*JB645, ZN-F*) of 106 Squadron. The bomber had taken off shortly after midnight with Pilot Officer E.C. Holbourn at the controls but nothing more was heard and the seven-man crew were later revealed to have all been buried in the Berlin 1939-1945 War Cemetery.

Bomber Command had two detached squadrons which worked as Special Duties units (138 and 161 Squadrons) dropping supplies and agents into occupied Europe. This was a very hazardous, but important, duty and many crews lost their lives. The squadrons also flew air-sea rescue operations, attempting to find airmen who had been unlucky enough to have come down in the sea. On the night of 23 January, 161 Squadron sent aircraft off on just such an operation. Two of its Halifax V aircraft failed to return and were presumed to have been unlucky enough to collide with one another over the North Sea, with the loss of all fourteen airmen aboard. The flight engineer in Halifax V (*LL182, MA-V*) was another Sunderland man, Sergeant Edward Robert Richardson (19). The airman left behind his parents, Edward and Bertha.[43]

While the commander of RAF Bomber Command, Sir Arthur Harris, was determined to press on with his campaign against German towns and cities, including the costly campaign against Berlin, his superiors also ordered him to attack specific targets because of vital German industries. On the night of 24/25 February he undertook such an attack on Schweinfurt in the south of Germany. This target had been identified as being crucial to the ball bearing manufacturing industry in Germany but was a very difficult target to locate and hit. American B-17 bombers had hit the town the previous day and Harris sent 734 of his bombers on this particular night. The tactics on this night were somewhat innovative, with the attacking force being split into two forces, one following the other two hours later in the hope that the enemy night-fighter force would not be able to cope. In many ways this worked, the leading force suffered the loss of twenty-two aircraft while the follow up force lost just eleven. Unfortunately, bombing was inaccurate, and it is believed little damage was done. Amongst the aircraft which failed to return was Halifax III (*LV778, C6-B*) of 51 Squadron, based at RAF Snaith. Pilot Officer D. Jackson had taken off shortly before 6.30pm but nothing more was heard from the crew until there was notification that they had been killed and buried at Durnach War Cemetery. The crew of eight men included yet another young, unmarried, Sunderland man, wireless operator/ air gunner, Flight Sergeant John Francis Brown (24).

On the night of 24 March, the weary crews of Bomber Command were briefed once more for Berlin. Unbeknownst to them, this would be the final raid on the city by the heavy bombers of the Command (although Mosquito raids would continue until the end of the war). The operation called for the use of 811 aircraft and became known in the Command as 'the night of the strong winds' as a powerful jet stream wind from the north blew many of the aircraft in the bomber stream off-track as they crossed Europe. Wind had not been forecast and, to compound difficulties, the methods used to warn navigators of wind changes failed to detect the change or diluted it as people back in England could not believe that such a strong wind was possible. With the bomber stream badly scattered, the lumbering bombers became even more vulnerable to fighter and flak attack as they could be singled out more easily by various radar aids. The raid did hit parts of Berlin (and beyond) and resulted in the bombing out of 20,000 people but it came at a terrible cost as 72 of the bombers failed to return to Britain. Of these, an estimated fifty were shot down by anti-aircraft fire (flak) while twelve of the remaining twenty were reported as having been shot down by night-fighters over the target. Amongst the aircraft lost were three Lancaster IIs from 115 Squadron based at RAF Witchford. Lancaster II (*DS678, KO-J*) had taken off at 6.49pm with Pilot Officer L.M. McCann, RCAF, at the controls. His wireless operator/air gunner was Sergeant William Bowey (21). The son of William Crossley Bowey and Elizabeth Bowey of Sunderland, he perished with four of his crew (two survived as

PoWs) when their Lancaster as shot down from 20,000ft by a night-fighter in the vicinity of Leipzig. The five men who died had, for many years, no known graves and are commemorated on the Runnymede Memorial but evidence recently came to light that Sergeant Bowey and his crewmates had been buried at Ohrdruf Cemetery, but subsequently lost. The panel on the Runnymede Memorial will be removed as they are now commemorated on special memorials at the Niederzwehren Cemetery, Kassel, with the inscription: 'WHO WAS BURIED AT THE TIME IN OHRDRUF CEMETERY, BUT WHOSE GRAVE CANNOT NOW BE FOUND. THEIR GLORY SHALL NOT BE BLOTTED OUT.'

It was not, of course, only the airmen of Bomber Command who were paying the price for the ongoing campaign against Germany. The men of 404 Squadron, RCAF, were mounting anti-shipping strikes daily. On 30 March, Sunderland lost yet another airman when the Beaufighter (*LZ297*) crashed into the sea during such a strike mission. The navigator was Flight Lieutenant Frederick Alan Kent (24).[44]

With Sir Arthur Harris keenly aware that he would shortly have to use his aircraft to support the build-up to D-Day and just as aware that the recent attempt to destroy Berlin had failed at a great cost in aircrew lives it seems that he was keen to have one final attack on a German city. The biggest problem with mounting such a raid on the night of 30/31 March was that it was now the full moon period during which the Command usually restricted itself to limited operations. Nevertheless, an early forecast of screening high-level cloud on the outbound route to Nuremburg in the far south of Germany resulted in his giving the command to attack that city with a force of 795 aircraft. The result was disastrous, with the heavy bombers not only not being screened by cloud but exposed by the light of a full moon and giving off distinctive vapour trails at the height they had been briefed to fly. Even worse, their straight route flew right over an enemy night-fighter assembly beacon; the result was carnage with ninety-six bombers being lost and ten more being stricken off charge upon their return. The loss of 545 aircrew was more than had been lost by Fighter Command during the entire Battle of Britain. Amongst those killed was Flying Officer Leslie Simpson (33) of 101 Squadron. The air gunner was a married man and left behind his widow, Marguerite, at their Fulwell home. Although 101 Squadron was flying normal bomber operations, it was a specialised squadron and had been issued with a specialised device known as ABC, which helped to jam enemy communications, and necessitated the addition of an extra, German-speaking, crewman as a special operator. Unfortunately, it would seem that it could also be tracked by some enemy radar systems and made the Lancasters of the squadron more vulnerable. On the night of the Nuremburg raid, 101 Squadron suffered the loss of no fewer than seven of its aircraft. Amongst them was Lancaster I (*LL832, SR-K2*) which took off from RAF Ludford Magna shortly after 10.00pm under the command of Flight Sergeant G. Tivey. Pilot Officer Simpson was the mid-upper gunner in the crew. The Lancaster, unlike so many on this raid, did not fall victim to a night-fighter but was shot down by flak, crashing near the village of Rubenach with the loss of all eight crewmen.[45]

With the demand for landing craft in the build-up to an invasion of Western Europe and the continuing demands of the RN, the decision was taken to expand production. William Pickersgill & Sons Ltd. sought and received Admiralty assistance in reopening the neighbouring yard which had belonged to John Priestman & Co., but which had been defunct since 1934. After refurbishment, the company began work on the construction of a variety of landing craft and took on orders for several naval vessels. The three Castle-class corvettes which had been started in 1943 were also transferred to the new yard. HMS *Leeds Castle* was completed in February, HMS *Morpeth Castle* in July and HMS *Nunney Castle* in October.[46]

During 1944, the yard began work on three Bay-class anti-aircraft frigates: HMS *Largo Bay*, HMS *Morecambe Bay,* and HMS *Mounts Bay*. Although laid down in 1944 none of the ships saw service during the war with the first two ships not being completed until early 1946.[47] HMS *Mounts Bay* was

HMS Leeds Castle *in April in April 1944 (Public Domain)*

HMCS Bowmanville *during the war (Public Domain)*

HMS Morpeth Castle *in 1944 (Public Domain)*

completed in 1949 and, like her sister ship, HMS *Morecambe Bay*, saw active service during the Korean War.[48]

On the night of 7 November, the blackout claimed yet another victim when Mrs Nellie Brandt of Peel Street was found lying in the street suffering from head injuries and shock. The unfortunate Mrs Brandt had apparently fallen over a low wall which she had failed to see in the blackout. She was admitted to Sunderland Royal Infirmary for treatment.

CHAPTER 7

1945: Victory and Peace

❖

What was to be the final year of the war opened with most people in Sunderland anticipating victory but well aware that although it appeared that Germany was on its knees and might capitulate in the coming weeks or months. The war with Japan was, if not in the balance, still being fought brutally and it appeared more than possible that the Japanese, fighting fanatically, might fight to the last and that the fighting might well go on, bloodily and with increasing loss of life, into the next year. For those with loved ones fighting against the Japanese, the thought of losing a loved one so late in the war was particularly worrying. For those who had loved ones who were prisoners of the Japanese there was even more uncertainty. It had become well known that the Japanese were treating their prisoners with great brutality and the uncertainty over how they might react faced with ultimate defeat was very concerning.

For some others – those with loved ones as prisoners of the Germans – the early months of the year brought some news of prisoners being released by the advancing allied armies. In early May, for example, the long-suffering but undeterred Wing Commander Kayll, DSO, DFC, was released from PoW camp and, after his return to Britain, was released from the RAF as a wing commander as well as being Mentioned in Dispatches.[49]

By this stage it was clear that Germany was beaten and, for several weeks, speculation had raged as to when the news of Victory in Europe Day would come. Like elsewhere, people had been hoarding their rations and making preparations for street parties and celebrations when the news did come. When the day did come, two public holidays were declared for 8 and 9 May, a large number of Sunderland shipyard workers were caught out and duly turned up for work as normal, only to find the works closed. On every street, bunting and flags appeared, and at the east end of the town near to the old barracks, a large bonfire was assembled topped by a suspended Guy, dressed as Hitler, complete with German helmet. The only dampener on the day, apart from the weather, was the shortage of beer in the town which resulted in many pubs running out and being forced to close.

The mayor (Councillor John Young), members of the council and other dignitaries listened to the prime minister's broadcast on VE Day at the town hall. After listening to the broadcast, the

The mayor and (l-r) Alderman F. Wilson and Mrs Wilson, Mr T. Wilkinson, Mrs T.R. Ridley, Mrs N. Waters, councillors Heil and Ridley, the Mace Bearer and Councillor N. Waters listen to the victory broadcast (Newcastle Journal)

mayor proclaimed the good news of the victory from the steps of the town hall. Despite rather inclement conditions a large crowd had assembled to hear the happy news before they embarked on their own celebrations.

The mayor later sent a telegram of congratulation to the prime minister and followed this up by moving a resolution at a meeting of the town council which pledged Wearside's loyalty and congratulated the king and queen on the successful conclusion of the war in Europe.

Like most communities, the people of Sunderland and the surrounding area welcomed VE Day with celebrations including street parties, dances and bonfires but there was also, for many, a sense of grief over the loss of a loved one during the course of the war. Sunderland had paid a heavy price with many of its men and women serving in the armed forces. The celebrations, when compared to many other areas, were actually quite muted in Sunderland with the local press describing them as being reserved, since many Wearsiders felt that it was perhaps too early to celebrate raucously while many men were still away facing the enemy.

At Hendon, the second day of the public holiday brought about a tragedy as a young Sunderland man drowned. Norman Young (17) was an apprentice carpenter who lived at Regent

The Mayor proclaims the news of victory from the steps of the Town Hall (Newcastle Journal)

Terrace, Sunderland. A friend, Robert Stormont (17) of Barbara Street, Sunderland, described how he had seen Norman, who was swimming about 20 yards from the beach, twice try to haul himself out of the water onto a sewage outlet pipe but on each occasion he was swept further out to sea by the waves. Several hours later, the unfortunate lad's body was found washed up on Hendon Beach by William Thomas Green of Henry Street East, Sunderland.

Although there was relief that the war in Europe was over, there were many Sunderland families who still faced an anxious time as they waited for news of loved ones who were involved in the fighting against the Japanese or had been taken prisoner of the Japanese earlier in the war.

With the news that the USA had dropped atomic bombs on Japan it was widely expected that the Japanese too would surrender and, indeed, the news was announced, making 15 August VJ Day. Once again, two days' public holiday was declared and the people of Wearside rejoiced with many looking forward to the return of loved ones, although for others the celebrations were still tinged with uncertainty and anxiety as they awaited news of the fate of those who were prisoners of the Japanese. Amongst those who had been taken prisoner were the men of the 125th Anti-Tank Regiment, Royal Artillery. The 250-strong unit had been initially formed at South Shields but had quickly moved to Dykelands Road Drill Hall and Seaburn Camp under the command of Lieutenant Colonel J. Dean. The 125th Regiment served for a while in England, including sterling service on the docks of Liverpool during the blitz on that city.

They sailed for India in October 1941 but were diverted to Singapore. Their arrival was tragic as their vessel, the *Empress of Asia*, was heavily bombed and ran aground on a reef, blazing furiously at the south end of Singapore. The discipline of the regiment meant that they were able to land with the loss of only one officer, Lieutenant Wilson. They were issued with rifles and rushed into the line to reinforce the infantry, even though it was absolutely hopeless. The survivors of the 125th Regiment, along with almost 100,000 others, were taken prisoner by the Japanese.

Officers of 125th Regiment (Sunderland Echo)

For the survivors this was the beginning of years of horror as they were put to work by the Japanese in horrendous conditions and brutal treatment. It was known that the unit had been split up in different camps and that at least forty-four of the men had already lost their lives (fifteen when a Japanese transport was sunk) and others had not been heard of since the fall of Singapore.

The reaction to the announcement of the Japanese surrender and final victory was in sharp contrast to that which had met VE Day. Within minutes of the midnight announcement, thousands of people invaded Fawcett Street amidst the anticipation of a speech from the mayor on the steps of the town hall at 1.00am. The happy throngs waited patiently and passed the time by singing songs and making merry. In fact the mayor had initially decided that, due to the timing of the announcement, he would make his speech at 11.00am but a telephone call from councillors, who were already at the town hall and had seen the crowds, brought him from his bed. The crowds were growing increasingly impatient and chanting of 'We want the mayor' had broken out, leading to Councillor George Potts making an announcement via loudspeaker that the mayor was on his way.

The crowd was so large that the mayor decided to make his speech from the balcony and when he appeared, loud and sustained cheering broke out causing him to wait for a full three minutes until he could begin speaking. In what seemed a rather uninspired address, he told them that the news had brought great joy, making an especial mention of the many Sunderland men who had been taken prisoner at the fall of Singapore. He concluded by asking the people of Sunderland to 'join in suitable celebrations' and to give thanks to God.

With the large crowd dispersing to begin a round of house parties, the police were called to rescue a lad who had climbed onto a ledge opposite the town hall, only to find that he could not get back down from his perch.

In the east end of the city, large crowds had also gathered and there were many bonfires erected and lit, while in other areas such as Pallion, Deptford and the Ford Estate, large celebratory crowds were celebrating by firing off fireworks. The mayor, together with the borough treasurer, toured all these areas to address the crowds and was warmly welcomed in each area. It was after 4.00am when he returned home. Following a request from the mayor, councillors Potts and Wilkinson made similar tours of areas which lay north of the river.

Musical performances were to the fore in the celebrations. At Mackie's Corner, where corporation workmen were repairing the tram lines, residents who were keen to celebrate brought a piano into the street, and the workmen found themselves being accompanied by a local resident who was highly successful in organising community singing. In Frederick Street, a one-man band led the crowds in an impromptu dance through the street. In many areas, private cars toured the streets, with people waving and cheering from their open sunroofs.

In Fulwell, crowds began assembling shortly after midnight with early celebrations being accompanied by the sounds of railway and pit hooters. In some ways the scenes were reminiscent of the first-footing associated with New Year as people visited friends and family. People shook hands in the streets, danced around the many bonfires and bellowed patriotic songs into the

Victory flags over Bridge Street (Sunderland Echo)

Cheering Wearsiders outside Sunderland Town Hall at 1.00am on VJ-Day (Sunderland Echo)

Sunderland residents with a sailor on VJ-Day (Sunderland Echo)

Celebrating Wearsiders give the victory salute for the camera (Sunderland Echo)

early morning darkness. A scene of particular jollity was the immediate area around the fire station and it was not until dawn that the crowds finally left for bed.

Those who had retired to bed and had not heard the joyous news were soon awakened by the cheering crowds or by the sounds of ships' hooters as ships in the South Docks sounded off and fired red flares into the night sky. Those who were crossing the Wearmouth Bridge could see the many bonfires bursting into light across the town.

For those wishing to give thanks in a less noisy and more reverent manner there was the option of church. St Peter's on Green Street was the first church in the town to open its doors and several people took the opportunity to quietly give thanks. St Peter's was also the first church to begin sounding its bells in celebration of the victory and the end of seven years of war.

By 2.30am, the crowds were thinning considerably, although many still roamed the streets singing and celebrating. Many others had gone to celebrate in their homes or those of friends or family while still more had retired to bed or to make plans for the celebrations that the day and the following day would surely bring. In High Street East, the crowds lasted longer than most at an impromptu street party but by 3.30am most had retired, tired but happy, to bed. One woman, returning home, tired, was overheard to remark: 'Hinny, let them enjoy themselves. This doesn't happen often, you know.'[50]

As had happened on VE Day, some workers, who seemingly had not heard the news, turned up for work as usual but were quickly apprised of the situation and turned away so they too could partake in the celebrations.

At 10.30am, crowds once again began to assemble outside the town hall where they were entertained by the police band. The crowds had been informed that the mayor would be making a second announcement and they filled in the time by dancing and singing aloud to the selection of tunes. With the clock tower bell still chiming 11 o'clock, the mayor and mayoress, accompanied by the robed town clerk, appeared on the balcony to great cheers and a fanfare of trumpets. Broadcasting equipment had been hurriedly fitted and, through this, the mayor told the crowds that, at last, the tragedy of what had been a long and drawn-out war had finally ended. He explained how the surrender had been unconditional and this was proper as Britain would have accepted nothing less after the tragedies that had been suffered over the previous years. He then expressed the hope that the children of the people of Sunderland would 'never again know the horrors of war'. After praising the contribution of Sunderland men and women in the services, the mayor reserved especial praise for the local industries. 'Sunderland industry', he said, 'men who stood by and worked day and night at the anvil, at the machine to forge the weapons and ships to bring victory and smash Japan'. His remarks were met with loud cheers causing him to pause. When he continued, he moved to more sombre thoughts, saying that the people remembered 'too, those who bear the marks of battle or were in hospital and those men and women of Sunderland, yes, the children too, who had given their lives'. While urging the people to celebrate, he also reminded them of the sacrifices that had been made and that many Sunderland families had experienced tragedy and loss. Speaking on these issues he said, 'Let's have some tea-parties. Let's have some tea and cake out on the tables, but let us remember in these moments those brave Sunderland men who have given their lives for their country.'

Others were more concerned with propriety being maintained. Alderman D. Cairns, presiding at Sunderland Magistrates' Court said that he hoped that the people of the town 'would be restrained in their rejoicings and would not be unruly during the celebrations'.[51] This was perhaps in reaction to the news that revellers had been blamed for a fire in the early hours, which had destroyed a large quantity of straw in a truck standing in the LNER siding near Sunderland Moor. This had not, however, been a deliberate act of vandalism as the fire service determined that it had been started by a spent rocket falling into the wagon.

As the morning went on, announcements were made regarding the organisation of celebratory events. Many street parties were being planned and it was announced that dancing was being organised at various locations such as at Seaburn, where the police band would provide musical accompaniment at the Cat and Dog steps, at the Town Moor and in Mowbray Park. Many churches also announced services, while the Solemn Benediction was said and followed by the singing of the 'Te Deum' in all Roman Catholic churches and a solemn High Mass planned for Sunday, 19 August. Bishopwearmouth Church planned a special town's service which took place on 3.00pm, preceded by a formal procession of public bodies from the town hall. Many public buildings were floodlit in the dark hours, a novelty after years of blackout. They included Bishopwearmouth Church and the Cenotaph.

Licensed premises were told that they were only permitted to open at the usual hours but the supply of beer was still a big concern for many licensees and imposed restraints of its own on the celebrations. Most businesses and shops rose to the occasion and decorated their premises with patriotic symbols and flags, while the bunting once again fluttered over the streets. The mayor also made a special appeal to those employed in the bakery trade to remain at work so that supplies could be obtained for the

One of the most attractive victory spectacles in Sunderland is Bishopwearmouth Church illuminated by floodlighting.

A flood-lit Monkwearmouth Church on VJ-Day (Sunderland Echo)

many street parties being planned. This was in response to a rush on the shops after several bakers decided to close. The grocers of Sunderland were exceptionally busy throughout the morning and the Grocers' Association asked members to remain open all day and through the next day, advising them to take their own holiday on 27 and 28 August. The Butchers' Association made a similar decision but asked members to delay their own celebrations until early September. Many public buildings and services remained closed for the two days of celebration. This included all welfare centres, the public libraries, and the museum and art gallery. It was also announced that children returning to school after the holidays would be awarded with a medal to commemorate the entry into universal peace.

The celebrations were far more evident than had been the case during VE Day, according to the press, but were somewhat dampened, once again, by poor weather, with frequent rain and a downpour on the first night of the celebrations. The second day was a little better but there were still frequent showers.

The *Sunderland Echo* also urged people not to forget the efforts of housewives during the war, telling readers that they had sacrificed much during the war years and continued to do so. Housewives, it declared, had for years put up with queuing, battling with tradesmen over rations, done their best with left-overs, kept an eye on coupons, 'and suffered the heartache of family separation'.[52] Even with the coming of VJ Day, the housewife was working, throwing her efforts into ensuring that the many parties had sufficient food to celebrate over the two-day holiday.

The family of Lieutenant Charles Alex Thwaites, RNVR, had especial reason to join in the celebrations as it was announced on VJ Day that the sailor, from Seaham, had been awarded the DSC for outstanding services in the Aegean Sea and for his part in assisting the clearing of the islands around Greece.

The cinemas maintained their popularity throughout the celebrations as people attended not only for the features but also to see newsreels of celebrations elsewhere, especially those in London featuring the Royal Family and other dignitaries. The people of Sunderland had a wide choice. The Regal was showing Dorothy Lamour in *A Medal for Benny*, the Royal featured Joan Fontaine in *The Constant Nymph*, at the Havelock it was *Keys of the Kingdom* starring Gregory Peck, while the Palace offered *Blithe Spirit* with Rex Harrison and the Ritz offered Judy Garland in *Meet Me in St Louis*. For those who wished for a more exuberant experience, the New Rink was hosting Grand Victory Dances with musical accompaniment provided by Jimmy Bain and his Band.

The second day and night of the victory celebration was somewhat affected by the heavy rain which fell, but dances still took place at the Moor,

Lieutenant (Temp) Charles Alex Thwaites, DSC (Sunderland Echo)

Advert for the Regal, Royal and the New Rink (Sunderland Echo)

Mowbray Park and Roker, while bonfires once again sprang up throughout the town with children making widespread use of 'spare' timber from bombed sites. On the 'highly respectable' Park Avenue estate in Seaburn, dignity was thrown to the wind as wood was gathered from any available source and a large bonfire lit, around which people of all ages danced and made merry to

Advert for the Havelock and Palace (Sunderland Echo)

Advert for the Ritz (Sunderland Echo)

the sounds of the exploding fireworks acquired in preparation for the big day.

Tea parties were a common theme throughout the day and while some took place inside homes the vast majority were out on the streets where neighbours mingled happily and collected together their rations to make the parties go with a swing. Many of the parties had musical accompaniment provided by various means. Some of the larger parties took place at Melbury Court, Fulwell, Acklam Avenue and Aysgarth Avenue in Grangetown, and at 2 Toward Road and 195 Cleveland Road. While many parties bravely went ahead others had to be postponed as heavy rain fell, making outdoor celebrations impossible.

Children in fancy dress at the Aysgarth Avenue street party (Sunderland Echo)

Revellers round a bonfire at a bombed site near Mowbray Park (Sunderland Echo)

Street tea party at St Aidan's Avenue (Sunderland Echo)

So, it was over. The people of Sunderland, battered and war weary were now faced with the expectation of welcoming back loved ones but also with the more daunting prospects of an uncertain future in which there would have to be a huge rebuilding programme along with efforts to make a fairer and more equitable society in Britain. While the authorities were already beginning the planning process there was a brief time for reflection on the achievements of Wearside during the war.

Sunderland had made many contributions to the war effort. From factory works producing specialised equipment for the armed forces to small firms engaged in work for the Air Ministry, the coal miners, the vast numbers of men from the area who served in the merchant navy, the equally large numbers who volunteered for service with the armed forces, in nursing, ARP, the Home Guard, etc. Undoubtedly, one of the greatest and most important contributions to the national war effort had been made by the shipyards and repair yards of the Wear.

The massive contribution of shipbuilding work on the Wear was led by W. Doxford & Sons Ltd. Through the course of the war, the massively expanded workforce and facilities had managed to complete a total of seventy-five merchant ships totalling over 500,000 tons. This enormous contribution to the war effort required huge commitment on the part of management and workforce but also a vast logistical effort which saw approximately 40,000 tons of steel being consumed by the yard each year.

Joseph L. Thompson & Sons Ltd. had survived a difficult period during the 1930s by utilising their innovation in ship design to produce the Thompson Economy steam tramp in the middle of that depression-shrouded decade. During the war, the company made a very significant contribution to the war effort by producing an output of forty ships totalling almost 277,700 tons and had played a large role in the development of the famed 'Liberty' ship design. In addition to its contribution to the war effort mentioned above, the yard also built an additional seven tramps, two cargo-liners (the *Chinese Prince* in 1943 and the *Silveroak* in the following year) and four 'intermediate', 5,000 ton, tankers for private owners during the war. After suffering heavy damage during the air raid of 24 May 1943, the yard was repaired and, in addition to those vessels mentioned above, managed to launch three fast cargo-liners for a government order.

Sir James Laing & Sons Ltd. achieved a magnificent record of production during the war and with the firm's specialism in the construction of tankers made a significant contribution to the war effort. The Deptford yard produced forty-one vessels during the war, thirty-two of them being tankers. Twenty-eight of these tankers were produced for government orders. Fifteen of these tankers were of the 'Norwegian' type of 14,700 tons, eight were 'Intermediate' types of 5,000 tons and the remaining five were of the 'Fast Oiler' type of 12,000 tons. In addition to these government orders, the firm also constructed three 'Norwegian' types and one 'Fast Oiler' type for private owners. Eight tramp vessels were also constructed during the war. One was built to government order, with the remaining seven being contracted by private owners. In addition, a fast cargo-liner, the *Empire Paragon*, was launched in 1944.

Short Brothers Ltd. completed twenty-eight tramps during the course of the war, of which twenty-four were government orders. The firm also built two small motor tankers for service in the Far East and a tank-landing craft for the Admiralty.

W. Pickersgill & Sons Ltd. had also suffered during the 1920s and 1930s and the yard had been closed between 1930 and 1935. Wartime production at the main yard consisted of twenty-two merchant ships. These included eight 'Empire' type tramps for government order, along with two smaller tramps, and twelve tramps for private owners. Alongside this production was the output of the defunct Priestman yard which the company took over with Admiralty assistance and which constructed frigates and landing craft.

Bartram & Sons Ltd. also saw an extremely busy war with massive construction targets being achieved. Wartime production amounted to some twenty-four ships. Nine tramps were built to government orders along with nine 'Empire' type vessels and one ship being built as a repair ship for RN service in the Far East. Private orders accounted for the remaining six ships.

Appendix A

❖

Known Locations of Bombs Dropped during Raid of 24 May 1943.

Type of Device[53]	Exploded or UXB	Location	Weight
HE	ex	Promenade, Roker Terrace	50kg
HE	ex	On Beach	50kg
HE	ex	Lower Promenade	250kg
HE	ex	On Beach	
HE	ex	On Beach	
HE	ex	On Beach	
IB		On Beach	500kg
IB		5, Dacre Road	500kg
HE	ex	In field east of Shields Road	500kg
PM	uxb	3, Newington Court	
PM	uxb	54, Eglinton Street	
HE	ex	Bonnersfield	500kg
HE	ex	Bonnersfield	500kg
PM	ex	J.L. Thompson's Shipyard	
PM	ex	In river near above location	
HE	ex	High Street West	1000kg
HE	ex	Dun Cow Street	1000kg
HE	ex	Cameron's Brewery, Dunning Street	250kg
HE	ex	South-east corner Fawcett Street	500kg
PM	uxb	Corby Hall	

PM	ex	Playing field, Corby Hall	
PM	uxb	150 yards south of Newlands Avenue.	
HE	ex	Almshouses, Littlegate	500kg
HE	ex	North Dock Road	50kg
HE	ex	Promenade, near Coast Guard Station	50kg
HE	ex	Devonshire Street	500kg
HE	ex	Abbs Street	500kg
PhIB	ex	Sans Street	
FP	ex	Upper Sans Street	
HE	ex	Walton's Lane	50kg
FP	ex	Fenwick's Brewery, Coronation Street	
FP	ex	Fenwick's Brewery, Coronation Street	
FP	ex	Rickaby Street	
FP	ex	Embankment near Barrack Road	
HE	ex	North Eastern Marine, South Docks	500kg
HE	ex	In sea in front of North Eastern Marine	
PhIB	ex	South Pier	
HE	ex	Hendon Dock, outside Monsanto Works	250kg
HE	ex	Hendon Dock, outside Monsanto Works	250kg
HE	ex	In Monsanto Works	250kg
HE	ex	West of Hudson Dock Bridge	50kg
HE	ex	Outside No 31 Coal Staith, Hendon Dock	50kg
HE	ex	West of Robson's Saw-mills	500kg

FP	ex	Hartley Street	
HE	ex	Town Moor	250kg
HE	ex	Octagon Cottage Road	250kg
HE	ex	Wear Street	500kg
HE	ex	D'Arcy Street	500kg
HE	ex	D'Arcy Road	250kg
HE	ex	Burlington Road	500kg
PM	ex	Salem Avenue	
HE	ex	Back Park Place West	500kg
HE	ex	Toward Road	50kg
HE	ex	Robinson Street	500kg
HE	ex	Mainsforth Terrace	500kg
HE	ex	Corporation Road	50kg
HE	ex	Lodge Terrace	250kg
HE	ex	Villette Path	50kg
HE	ex	Stratford Avenue	1000kg
HE	ex	On railway, Hetton Sidings, Ayre's Quay	50kg
HE	ex	Near Black Swan Hotel, Silksworth Row	50kg
FP	ex	Trimdon Street – Rose Street	
HE	ex	Hedley Street	500kg
HE	ex	Ravensworth Street	500kg
HE	ex	Pallion New Road, near Alexandra Bridge	250kg
HE	ex	Bishopwearmouth Cemetery	250kg
HE	ex	Bishopwearmouth Cemetery	250kg
HE	ex	St George's Square	1000kg
PM	ex	Gorse Road	
PM	ex	Alexandra Road, near Eye Infirmary	
HE	ex	Hendon Gas Works	50kg

HE	ex	Railway at NE corner of Gas Works, Hendon	50kg
HE	ex	Near railway, 150 yds NE of Gas Works	50kg
HE	ex	Opposite 14, The Westlands	50kg
HE	ex	In roadway, Priory Grove	50kg
HE	ex	In roadway, Barnard Street	50kg
HE	ex	At rear of Barnard and Abingdon Streets	50kg
FP	ex	Oil Storage Tanks, S of North Tidal Basin	
HE	ex	North Eastern Marine Engine Works	250kg
HE	ex	Fell in Hendon Dock	
HE	ex	Fell in Hendon Dock	
PhIB	uxb	Direct hit on house junction of D'Arcy Tce and Fore St	
FP	ex	Direct hit on ship lying in North Tidal Basin	
HE or FP	ex	Fenwick's Brewery, North Durham St	50kg
HE	ex	Warren Street (in debris American Hotel)	50kg
HE	ex	Direct hit on ship in Hudson North Dock	1000kg
		Holed and sank a water-boat in Hudson Dock N.	
HE	ex	Wearmouth Colliery Drops	50kg
HE	ex	Near No 1 Post, Wearmouth Colliery	50kg
HE	ex	Field at rear of Ambleside Terrace	500kg
HE	ex	Vaux's Brewery	50kg
HE	ex	Cameron's Brewery	50kg

HE	ex	Promenade, Roker Terrace	50kg
HE	ex	On Beach	50kg
HE	ex	Lower Promenade	250kg
HE	ex	On Beach	
HE	ex	On Beach	
HE	ex	On Beach	
IB		On Beach	500kg
IB		5, Dacre Road	500kg
HE	ex	In field east of Shields Road	500kg
PM	uxb	3, Newington Court	
PM	uxb	54, Eglinton Street	

Notes

1. The MV *British Prudence* was sunk in the Western Atlantic on 23 March 1942.
2. See, all by this author: *Newcastle upon Tyne at War, 1939-1945* (Pen & Sword, 2019); *Tynemouth & Wallsend at War, 1939-1945* (Pen & Sword, 2018); and *Edinburgh at War, 1939-1945* (Pen & Sword, 2018).
3. *Sunderland Echo*, 6 September 1939, p. 6.
4. The captain of U-47 was Gunther Prien and on this, his first, combat patrol the vessel sunk three British merchant ships. On 14 October, Prien and the U-47 found fame when they claimed to have been responsible for infiltrating the fleet harbour at Scapa Flow and sinking HMS *Royal Oak*. All of the crew from the SS *Rio Claro* survived their ordeal and were rescued.
5. *Newcastle Evening Chronicle*, 9 September 1939, p. 5.
6. *Sunderland Echo*, 11 September 1939, p. 3.
7. *Sunderland Echo*, 11 September 1939, p. 3.
8. HMS *Courageous* had begun life as a Courageous-class cruiser and had been launched in 1916 before taking part in the final two years of the First World War. Due to naval treaty rules she was converted into an aircraft carrier with the work being complete by 1928.
9. Stoker 1st Class White is commemorated on the Plymouth Naval Memorial. The SS *Kafiristan* was launched in 1924. The ship was owned by the Newcastle-based Common Bros. Ltd.
10. Aircraftman 1st Class Dixon is commemorated on the Runnymede Memorial.
11. Chief Engineer Mason is commemorated on the Tower Hill Memorial.

12. HMS *Port Quebec* continued as a minelayer until 1943 when she was again converted, this time into an aircraft repair ship, and renamed HMS *Deer Sound*. She finally began her commercial service in 1947 after being returned to Port Line.

13. *Sunderland Echo*, 5 March 1940, p. 1.

14. *Daily Mirror*, 8 March 1940, p. 26. The controversy rumbled on with the Lord Chancellor banning a performance at Cardiff on 11 March but shows later went ahead. Miss Dixey found fame and some notoriety in 1942 when she formed her own company of women and rented the Whitehall Theatre in London to put on a review entitled *The Whitehall Follies*. This was the first striptease show to be performed in London's West End and Miss Dixey remained at the Whitehall producing the *Peek-a-Boo Reviews* until 1947. Forced to retreat to the provinces in 1947 as audience tastes changed, Dixey could not adapt and retired, bankrupt, in the late 1950s. She died, aged just 50, in 1964. Dixey still managed to court controversy in 2011 when a plan by English Heritage to mount a blue plaque commemorating her outside her former home at Wentworth Court, Surbiton, was turned down by the residents' association due to the title 'Striptease Artiste' being used.

15. When the 2nd DLI reformed in Britain following its evacuation from Dunkirk there were only 180 men, comprised of survivors from D Company and the battalion's B echelon, along with a few scattered survivors, stragglers and wounded.

16. W.F. Blackadder had made a name for himself by scoring several victories during the Battle of France and finished the war as a wing commander at Allied Expeditionary Force HQ. During the war he was awarded the DSO and OBE, as well as being Mentioned in Dispatches. After the war he remained with the Auxiliary Air Force, commanding 607 Squadron until late 1948 when he became commanding officer of the Northumberland wing of the Air Training Corps. After leaving this post in 1951 he became director of

the Moor Line shipping company. He died on 21 November 1997.

17. *Shields Daily News*, 12 July 1940, p. 4.
18. None of the crew's bodies were ever recovered and they are commemorated on the Runnymede Memorial.
19. Pilot George Hall is commemorated on the Tower Hill Memorial. In 1948 the HM Survey vessel *Sharpshooter* located the wreck of the *Balzac* some 1,920 yards off the Roker lighthouse.
20. Shortly after this, the Luftwaffe repainted its rescue aircraft in camouflage and rearmed them. By the end of 1940 approximately forty of its air-sea rescue aircraft had been lost, twenty-five of them being shot down by RAF fighters. It has to be said that the Luftwaffe would also attack RAF rescue aircraft later in the war.
21. The dead and/or missing were: Hauptmann R. Stesszyn (the Staffelkapitan); Feldwebel W. Meyer (his body washed up on the Yorkshire coast); Gefreiter S. Zaunig; Gefreiter J. Perl.
22. *Sunderland Echo*, 26 July 1940, p. 3.
23. *Shields Daily News*, 25 October 1940, p. 4.
24. *Newcastle Journal*, 26 October 1940, p. 5.
25. *Sunderland Echo*, 20 June 1941, p.
26. *Ibid.*
27. *Ibid.*
28. *Sunderland Echo*, 30 September 1941, p. 4.
29. Mr Willey is buried at Sunderland (Monkwearmouth) Cemetery and it appears that his widow's claim regarding his death being related to wartime service was accepted as he is mentioned on the Commonwealth War Grave Commission website.
30. Both Ordinary Seaman Nutter and Leading Seaman Walshaw are commemorated on the Portsmouth Naval Memorial.
31. *Sunderland Daily Echo & Shipping Gazette*, 30 July 1942, p. 8.
32. Miss Thornton led a very varied life. Amongst her wartime claims to fame was as the first entertainer to land on the

Normandy beaches after the D-Day invasion. After the war, she became a successful cinema actress and one of Britain's first post-war sex symbols, changing her name to Christine Norden. In 1951 she starred in the comedy film *Reluctant Heroes* alongside her sister, June Mitchell (Elizabeth June Thornton). She settled in New York after moving to the USA in 1952 following her third marriage, to a US Air Force sergeant. She continued acting and also performed in Broadway plays and musicals such as *Tenderloin* and the comedy *Scuba Duba*. In the latter play she once again found fame, becoming the first actress to appear topless on Broadway. She returned to London in the 1970s although she retained an apartment in New York where she held several exhibitions of her paintings. She married for a fifth time in 1980 but died, aged just 63, following a heart bypass operation in 1988. Famed as a sex symbol Christine Norden's autobiography, *The Champagne Days are Over*, detailed her five marriages as well as a number of other romantic connections during her performing life.

33. *Sunderland Echo*, 10 November 1942, p. 2.

34. HMS *Manxman* underwent emergency repairs at Oran and Gibraltar before relocating to Newcastle where she was properly repaired. The minelayer was recommissioned on 10 April 1945 and dispatched to the British Pacific Fleet. She arrived shortly after VJ-Day and later took part in repatriation and supply duties before being scrapped in 1973.

35. The two Luftwaffe airmen recovered from the sea were: Unteroffizier K. Roos; and Unteroffizier B. Mittelstadt.

36. *Shields Daily News*, 17 May 1943, p. 5.

37. Dennis Johnson is commemorated on the Tower Hill Memorial.

38. Lieutenant Colonel Suga destroyed many of the records of the camps which he ran and, when captured, committed suicide rather than face the consequences of his brutal running of these camps.

39. See: https://www.thunder-and-lightnings.co.uk/memorial/ entry.php?id=121. The confusion may have arisen from the fact that although the Albemarle was an Armstrong Whitworth design it was largely constructed by A.W. Hawksley Ltd of Gloucester, a subsidiary of Gloster specifically formed for the Albemarle project. Gloster itself was part of the Hawker Siddeley group, which also included Armstrong Whitworth.

40. Leading Seaman Stokell is commemorated on the Plymouth Naval Memorial.

41. The *Empire Trail* survived the war and served for a variety of owners under a number of names after the war. As the *Ocean Glory* she was broken up and scrapped in Japan in 1963.

42. All of the crew are buried at Berlin 1939-1945 War Cemetery.

43. The crew of both aircraft were never found and are commemorated on the Runnymede Memorial. The other Halifax involved was *DG272, MA-U.*

44. Flight Lieutenant Kent is commemorated on the Runnymede Memorial.

45. All of the crew rest in the Rheinberg War Cemetery.

46. HMS *Leeds Castle* saw service protecting Atlantic convoys during the war. After the war she, along with others of her class, was converted into a frigate and took part in the fleet review to commemorate the coronation of HM Queen Elizabeth II in 1953. She also starred in the film *Cockleshell Heroes* in 1955 before she was scrapped three years later. HMS *Morpeth Castle* spent most of the war conducting anti-submarine exercises off Tobermory and Gibraltar. She was paid off in 1946 and broken up in 1960. HMS *Nunney Castle* was transferred to the control of the Royal Canadian Navy before completion and served as HMCS *Bowmanville* in the final years of the war. She was sold to a Chinese company for mercantile use in 1946. From 1949 she was rearmed and served the Communist-led government as the *Kuang Chou* before being struck off in 1986.

47. HMS *Largo Bay* saw brief service in the Mediterranean before being relegated to the Plymouth Reserve Fleet in August 1946. She took part in the fleet review to celebrate

the coronation of HM Queen Elizabeth II in 1953 before she was sold for scrap six years later. HMS *Morecambe Bay* saw active service during the Malayan Insurgency in 1949 and during the Korean War. She was sold to the Portuguese navy in 1961 and renamed the NRP *Dom Francisco de Almeida*. She was scrapped in 1970.

48. Like her sister ship, HMS *Mounts Bay* was also sold to the Portuguese navy in 1961. Renamed the NRP *Vasco da Gama* she was sold for scrap in 1971.

49. Wing Commander Joseph Robert Kayll, OBE, DSO, DFCAE, DL, returned to the family timber business but kept an interest in the Auxiliary Air Force, reforming 605 Squadron at Ouston. A keen yachtsman, he formed the Sunderland Yacht Club. He died on 3 March, 2000.

50. *Sunderland Echo*, 15 August 1945, p. 4.

51. *Sunderland Echo*, 15 August 1945, p. 8.

52. *Sunderland Echo*, 16 August 1945, p. 2.

53. HE: High Explosive; IB: Incendiary Bomb; PM: Parachute Mine; PhIB: Phosphorous Incendiary Bomb; FP: Fire Pot device.

Index